Prepared for the Wedding—
Prepared for the War!

The Bride Wears
Combat Boots

Lois A. Hoshor

The Bride Wears Combat Boots
by Lois A. Hoshor

ISBN 1-58169-008-8

For Worldwide Distribution
Printed in the U.S.A.

Companion Press
An Imprint of Genesis Communications, Inc.
P. O. Box 91011 • Mobile, AL 36691
(888) 670-7463
Email: GenesisCom@aol.com

Dedication

I would like to dedicate this book to my family, first of all, who have been a source of encouragement to me each step of the way. My husband Bob; the one who allowed me the *space* I needed to do what I had to do. My son John, who has been an example I have used many times as the godly husband and father a man should be. To my daughter Ginger, who has prodded, poked and at times pushed to get me to keep on, keeping on. She has truly been an inspiration during times when it seemed as though no one else *really* believed I could do it. I've always known she believed.

And my friend, Mikki, who was always there to listen when I would grumble and complain, and then tell me to get it together and go on with the plan of the Lord for my life. Thanks for keeping me out of Lazarus!

Without their help, I could not have accomplished the things I have done. It has truly been a body ministry.

Acknowledgements

We are a sum total of all the experiences, teachings, love and circumstances of life that have come our way. I have had the privilege of having had many influences touch me for the Lord. My Grandpa and Grandma Green, who were the Lord personified in my life for so long. My mother and father, Ginny and Merle Mason, through whom I learned that, though we may not always understand, God is always there. My sisters, Shirley and Judy, who helped me learn to pray and my brother Ron, who though not often there, is always there.

I can't forget my brother-in-law and friend, Ed Sharp, who has probably been my best sandpaper so far. Thanks to all of you for being who you have been in my life. Whether you want to admit it or not, you've helped make me what I am today, whatever that may be!

Table of Contents

Introduction

And I heard as it were the voice of a great multitude, and as the voice of many waters, and as the voice of mighty thunderings, saying, Alleluia: for the Lord God omnipotent reigneth. Let us be glad and rejoice, and give honor to Him: for the marriage of the Lamb is come, and His wife hath made herself ready. And to her was granted that she should be arrayed in fine linen, clean and white: for the fine linen is the righteousness of saints. And He saith unto me, Write, Blessed are they which are called unto the marriage supper of the Lamb. And He saith unto me, These are the true sayings of God (Revelation 19:6-9).

We can see, as we read these Scriptures, that God has a plan; and we, as His children, are an important part of that plan. We are the Bride of His only begotten Son, Jesus Christ. We are called His saints.

As you look at your own life, or at the lives of the church, you can't help but wonder how this will ever take place. "The wife has made herself ready," and yet we seem to be so far away from that description of His Bride.

I have for many years ministered to the Body of Christ many truths, and yet, as the Lord kept speaking to me to write this book, I had to wonder where the answers would come from. Was I capable of getting the message out in a way that would do the job He wanted done? I have seen many failures as well as successes over the years, and I realize my strength comes from Him. As I sit at my computer waiting for the right words to come, I tremble at the thought of the responsibility that comes with writing such a book. I will be judged with every word I write and will someday stand before the Lord to answer for them.

I finally came to the realization that this is the reason for my delay in putting these thoughts and what I consider revelation from the Lord into print.

I have found it is certainly true that the higher the call, the greater the price. I realize Jesus paid the price for our salvation and victory, but I have also found that we are expected to do our part. Faith with works will be required to fulfill God's plan and purpose for your life.

As a part of His many membered Body, I must walk in obedience to His call on my life. Though a son, I too will learn obedience through the things I suffer (Hebrews 5:8).

This, my fellow workers of the cross, is **The Bride Wearing Combat Boots!**

I pray the Lord will enlighten, feed and fill our hearts with His truths as we look at what it means to be the wife or church that *readies herself*.

Chapter 1

We're in a War!

My people are destroyed for lack of knowledge
(Hosea 4:6).

As I ponder how to start this book, I realize the Lord is not instructing me to write to the novice or baby in Christ. As you get into the teaching contained in these pages, you too will realize it is not for everyone.

There are many in the Church today who are just that—*in the church*. Then there are those who are busy with their works for the Lord: some called, some just busy. But there is another group of people who are being called apart, separated, changed and transformed into His likeness and image. These people are the *Bride of Christ*.

If you are in this group, you will know it. You are the ones being prepared for battle. You are the ones who are probably weary and in the constant state of battling fatigue. Without a doubt, you are wondering if there is any victory in sight.

If this sounds like you, then this book is for you. I want you to know: *you are in a war*!

****

I have found that one of the greatest weapons the enemy uses in the Body of Christ is *ignorance*. What does the Word of God have to say to us concerning this?

For we wrestle not against flesh and blood, but against principalities, against powers, against the rulers of the darkness of this world, against spiritual wickedness in high places (Ephesians 6:12).

1. Recognize the enemy

If Satan can keep you in ignorance of his ways and schemes, then he has a foothold in your life. We are not in a battle with our spouse, our boss, our children or our in-laws. The enemy is the *kingdom of darkness*.

2. Deception

We need to understand something. The devil doesn't have anything new to work with. He is still using the same old material he used on mankind in the Garden of Eden. He will lie to us, we believe the lie and are, therefore, deceived. Once that happens, defeat soon follows.

3. Rejection

Through believing the lie of the enemy, the door is

then opened to other spirits such as rejection, oppression and depression.

> *My people are destroyed for lack of knowledge: because thou hast rejected knowledge, I will also reject thee, that thou shalt be no priest to Me: seeing thou hast forgotten the law of thy God, I will also forget thy children.* (Hosea 4:6).

Hear what the Lord is saying! It is not the fact that knowledge wasn't available, but that the knowledge was *rejected.* Knowledge is there for any who will come. Look at the repercussions of that rejection: ". . . You shall be no priest to Me. . . and . . . I will also forget thy children."

It will not just affect you, but your children also. The knowledge of the Word of the Lord will bring victory and balance to our lives. We must know how the enemy works and the strategy of the Lord, for warfare is the only way to win the war!

We know who the enemy is, but *how does he work?*

Chapter Two

The Doorway to the Soul

Let this mind be in you, which was also in Christ Jesus (Philippians 2:5).

I had an experience shortly after I had left my job at a Christian television station to go into full-time evangelism. I was sitting at the kitchen table with my Bible open when the Holy Spirit asked me this question: "Where is Satan's rightful dwelling place?" I was so astounded at the Lord speaking so distinctly to me that I could hardly stay in my chair. I knew I didn't know the right answer to that question. I could have said all kinds of things that I had been taught about where Satan dwells, but I *just knew* that was not what the Lord wanted to hear.

I finally said, "Lord, I don't know what You want me to answer." He then spoke to my spirit and said for me to pay close attention to what He was about to say because it would be of great importance in the times ahead.

He began to reveal to me the functions of the human brain. Everything we have ever experienced is locked in

4

our brain, either in the conscious or subconscious realm. We are taught as a Christian that when we come to the Lord, all things become new. The old passes away and there is no more old man nature in us. The Holy Spirit began to reveal to me that the old, dead spirit becomes new, born again, and the soul is *being* renewed.

He then said the soul is made up of three parts: the mind, the will and the emotions. The only way the enemy can get to us is through the mind, or the doorway to the soul. He will plant a thought, our will comes into effect and we choose to act upon that thought one way or another.

Our emotions are then affected toward the good or the bad, depending upon the choice we make. At this time, our *soul* is being tested.

Remember, I said earlier that everything we have ever experienced is locked into our mind someplace. The Lord told me that when we are born again, our conscious mind is cleansed and we begin a new walk with Him. We have a new spirit, and all is well. All of a sudden, out of nowhere, a thought, word or action comes out of us and we wonder where it came from. We feel so guilty because a Christian shouldn't say or do such things. We repent, and think all is well. The next thing we know, another incident takes place, and we find ourselves in a constant battle and don't know why or what we are fighting against. The Lord said that these are the *dark areas of the soul*. Where is Satan's rightful dwelling place?

Anyplace Where There is Darkness

The subconscious mind is like a big computer: it has storage cells. The enemy is not dumb, as many would like to think. He simply bides his time, and at a moment of weakness, draws on old material that is stored in our mind.

I sat thinking about all of this. I must admit, my mind was boggled. I had never heard this taught. I had never so much as thought about such a thing, and the Lord was telling me to pay attention to what He is saying.

I asked the Lord to lead me to Scripture to back up what I heard Him saying. He led me to II Corinthians 10:4-5:

> *For the weapons of our warfare are not carnal, but mighty through God to the pulling down of strong holds; Casting down imaginations, and every high thing that exalteth itself against the knowledge of God, and bringing into captivity* every thought *to the obedience of Christ* (emphasis added).

The enemy gets into the camp through our mind. Our thoughts and our imagination are his playground, but our weapons are mighty through God. We are to *pull down the strongholds*!

The Lord then reminded me of the Scripture that says

we are destroyed because of lack of knowledge. He said His children are not aware of how the enemy works, and because of that fact, they are walking around in defeat.

I made some notes and prayed about all the Lord had said. I must admit, I was very apprehensive about what to do with this since it seemed so "far out" to me. The Lord assured me He would show me the truth of it in the days to come.

A few days later, a woman called me to ask if she could come for a counseling session. I told her I was not a trained counselor, and all I could do was listen and then pray for the Lord to give guidance. She said that was what she wanted, so we scheduled a meeting. She came to my house and, not knowing her, I waited for her to explain to me her problem. As a member of the Soul Seekers, I had been to her church to sing. She had also seen me on television, so she knew me more than I knew her. She said she knew I was spirit-filled although she was not. She did not attend a church that taught this experience.

She was hesitant to say very much about why she had come. She said her husband had gotten saved after several years of marriage and she thought everything was finally going to be good in their life and family. But then he told her he was ready to leave her. There was no other woman involved, so she was really confused. I asked her if she would be fearful if I prayed in the Spirit, not knowing how to pray effectively myself. She replied that it would be fine since she had heard people do that on Christian television. I asked the Lord to reveal to her, by the power of the Holy Spirit, what the root of the problem was, while I began to pray in the Spirit. Almost immediately, this woman began to wail and sob almost uncontrollably. I was at a loss to know what to do. I asked the Lord what I should do and He said, "*nothing* . . . just keep on praying." I was obedient. I had never seen anyone so totally overcome with emotion as she seemed to be.

This went on for about 15 minutes. When she finally raised her head from the table, she was a sight to see. Her face was swollen, and she looked like she had been beaten. She then said, "You will not believe what happened." I thought to myself, "You got that right, lady!" but I just listened. She said the minute I asked the Holy Spirit to reveal to her the root of the problem and started praying in the Spirit, she was instantly taken back to her childhood. She was five years old and her grandfather was molesting her. He died a few weeks after this happened, and she had never told anyone about it. It had been totally buried in her subconscious mind. She said the reason her husband was going to leave her was because of their sexual relationship. She had never responded to him in all the years they had been married, though they had birthed two children. He thought it was because she was a Christian and he wasn't. Then, when he accepted Christ and his life was so radically changed, nothing changed in their sexual relationship. He was ready to throw in the towel. The Lord showed her while I prayed that, in her mind, every time her husband reached for her, she was that little five year old and her husband was her grandfather.

She had buried in her all those years the fear that she had been the cause of her grandfather's death. She was so overwhelmed with the realization of what had happened, she didn't know what to do. The Lord then said, "These are dark areas of the soul."

What can pierce the darkness? *Light!* What is the Light? *Jesus Christ is the Light!*

I explained to her what the Lord had revealed to me a few days prior to this and told her we were going to speak the Light of Christ to permeate the darkness, and the darkness would have to go. Satan isn't given multiple choice when it comes to the power and Word of the Living God.

After I prayed for her, she spoke forth forgiveness to her grandfather for what he had done to her and asked the Lord to pierce the darkness with His light. She was *instantly transformed* before my eyes. I have never seen such a sight. The pain and hurt were gone, and a peace that truly passes understanding was visible upon her face. Her circumstances had not changed one bit, but her outlook had.

I prayed for her to receive the baptism in the Holy Spirit before she left. She called me the next day, and I hardly recognized her voice over the phone. She had praised the Lord in her new tongue all the way home.

That night she decided to prepare her husband's favorite dinner. She was sitting at the kitchen table when he came in from work. He went to the kitchen sink, took off his dirty, sweaty shirt, laid it on the counter (right next to the food being prepared), and began to wash his hands. This simple act had been a bone of contention between them from the time of their marriage. Why couldn't he go to the bathroom to wash his hands? She felt that old anger rise up inside and before she knew what had happened, the Holy Spirit spoke to her and said, "Look at the tired, sweaty muscles in that back. He does this for you and your children." All at once, a love she had never felt before rose up within her. She went over and put her arms around his waist, kissed him on the back and began to weep. This was the first time in all their years of marriage that she had ever reached out to touch him. Needless to say, their lives and marriage were transformed for the glory of Christ.

What Happened?

And ye shall know the truth and the truth shall make you free (John 8:32).

The strongholds of the enemy had been pulled down, and victory was the result. *The mind is the doorway to the soul.* What brought that freedom? Knowledge of the Truth! Not just *truth.* Truth has always been. It's *knowledge* of the Truth that brings us freedom.

Chapter 3

Know Your Weapons

For the weapons of our warfare are not carnal
(II Corinthians 10:4).

As a child of God, we have all heard about putting on the armor of God. You can read about this in Ephesians 6:10-17. Paul starts this passage of Scripture by exhorting the brothers in Christ to "be strong in the Lord and in the power of His might." This tells us right from the start where our strength comes from. Verse 13 tells us to put on the whole armor of God. Why? That we may be able to withstand in the evil day and having done all, to stand.

Why are so many Christians floundering around like fish out of water? Because they are trying to fight a spiritual battle with weapons of the flesh. Or if they are using weapons God has provided, they just put on part of them.

Your loins *must* be girded with truth; your heart *must* be covered with the breastplate of righteousness; your feet *must* be shod with the preparation of the gospel of peace; you *must* have on the helmet of salvation; you *must* have the sword of the Spirit, which is the Word of God; and above all, you *must* take the shield of faith with which you will be able to quench *all* the fiery darts of the wicked.

Notice something here. He didn't say to do this just in case you get into a battle. He didn't say to do this because there *might* be an enemy out there somewhere just waiting to *maybe* attack you. He didn't say to do this as a faith exercise. . . "But don't worry, you won't ever need to use any of your weapons." *No!*

He did say, "In the world you shall have tribulation" (John 16:33b). This is a promise of God. We *are* in a war, so *know your weapons.*

The Lord said in Luke 19:13 that we are to *occupy* until He comes. That is a military term which actually means to go behind enemy lines and take back the ground that has been taken from you.

How Can We Do This?

We've been told what our weapons are. What other tools has the Lord provided for us? What is some of the ground that has been taken from us by the enemy that we are to go after and occupy?

The number one request I am given to pray for is lost loved ones: those that have never known the Lord or have known Him and backslidden or fallen away from Him.

But if our gospel be hid, it is hid to them that are

lost: In whom the god of this world hath blinded the minds of them which believe not, lest the light of the glorious gospel of Christ, who is the image of God, should shine unto them (II Corinthians 4:3-4).

Another weapon of our warfare is prayer. Just any kind of prayer? *No!* What, then, is the answer to the problem of the enemy stealing our loved ones, blinding their minds so the Gospel of Jesus Christ does not get through to them? We must learn how to pray *effectively*. We *must* learn the difference between praying words and praying *the* Word.

Pray that the Lord of the harvest will send workers into their field. Pray their minds be unblinded, for the god of this world has blinded them lest they see the salvation of the Lord.

Go behind the enemy lines and take back that which the enemy has stolen from you! Your *family, finances, health*—find the Word that fits your situation and effectively pray that Word.

Know what your weapons are and how to use them effectively against the enemy. Praise God!

We're going to look at the power of prayer in a deeper way and find out just what the Lord has put at our disposal as a weapon against the enemy and how great the effect of that weapon can be in our lives.

Chapter 4

Missiles of Intercession

The effectual fervent prayer of a righteous man availeth much (James 5:16b).

In the first chapter of Genesis, God gave power and dominion over the things of this world to the man He created. When man fell, that power was given to Satan. A contract was signed with the juice from a fruit tree, and the time allotted for that contract was set from the very beginning. Until that time is fulfilled, God *cannot* and *will not* move in and take that authority from Satan *unless some of His children ask Him to do it.* That gives God the legal right to interfere with the workings of the devil. The power of the shed Blood, the work done at Calvary, the name of Jesus, and His resurrection, gave us the *right* to ask. Jesus took the power of sin, the keys to the Kingdom, and gave them to us. But, if we don't use them, *nothing will be done*!

How Can We Interfere
With the Work of the Devil?

Through prayer! There are all kinds of prayer. There is the prayer of faith, the prayer of consecration, the prayer of worship, the prayer of agreement, praying in the Spirit, and the prayer of intercession: They all produce different results. What we need to learn is *how* to pray and *when*.

The church world has made a big mistake in not teaching, or sometimes even understanding, the various ways to pray. Because of this fact, many of our prayers are going unanswered. We have been taught to close every prayer with "if it be Thy will," because this is the way Jesus prayed. However, there is only one example of this in the Bible and that is in the Garden of Gethsemane when He was praying the prayer of consecration. When we are praying for our lost loved ones to be saved, we don't need to tack that onto the end of the prayer because we *know* what the Lord's will is concerning their salvation. He would that none should perish but all come to the saving knowledge of who He is (I Peter 3:9). That is His Word! When we are seeking the Lord for healing, we need to realize that His Word says He paid the price for our healing to be received. There are certain rules that apply to certain needs being met, and we need to go to the rule book (the Bible) to find out which ones to use when.

One thing I have learned in the last few years is that

God cannot be put in a box and shipped out like merchandise sent U.P.S. Sometimes we need to call the elders and anoint with oil. Other times we need to stand in faith and know the answer is on the way. To get the results we need, we *must* learn the right way to pray. Let's look at *intercession* and the power that it contains.

We know from the book of Hebrews that Jesus is our High Priest, ever interceding for us. We can also see in John 17 that Jesus prayed for us when He was here on this earth. Isn't that an awesome thought? Jesus, the Son of God, prayed for you!

We, on the other hand, don't always know *how* to pray. Romans 8:26 says:

Likewise the Spirit also helpeth our infirmities; for we know not what we should pray for as we ought: but the Spirit itself maketh intercession for us with groanings which cannot be uttered.

We have all kinds of examples of intercessors in the Bible. We have Moses interceding for the people. We have Aaron and Hur interceding for Moses. We see David, Abraham, Daniel, Paul, Esther, Deborah and many others being used in intercession. Some of the characteristics of intercession are *pleading, intense, unselfish* and *victorious*.

Jesus is, of course, our prime example. Scripture says in Hebrews 7 that He lives to make intercession for us.

How much more should we be interceding for the Bride of Christ to ready herself?

Intercession does not change God. God never changes. Intercessional prayer changes people, including ourselves, and it changes circumstances. It will also change *our response* to the circumstances; that is what brings victory.

Intercession means to make a plea for someone else. We are going to look at a few examples of intercession and the results it brought.

Several years ago, I held a seminar called Praise and Worship and the Power of Intercession. At this meeting was a young woman who had accepted the Lord as a young girl, but had not matured in any way since her initial experience. As I was closing out the teaching, the Lord gave a word of knowledge concerning someone who needed three things to take place in her life. She needed to be filled with the Holy Ghost; she needed a miracle of healing in her body; and her marriage was on the rocks. Only the Lord could give her what she needed. As this woman responded to the Word of the Lord, a miracle took place. She was healed, filled with the Holy Spirit and the Lord placed within her what she needed to be able to forgive and love her husband.

She listened to my teaching tapes on prayer and intercession and began to apply them to her life. She began to lift up her lost loved ones to the Lord, in faith believing it was His will they be saved. Within two years time, her marriage was healed, her husband received a hunger for the Lord, her family began to come into the knowledge of who Jesus Christ is and miracle after miracle had taken place in her family.

Why? Because she heard, believed and stood upon the Word of the Living God. She had a revelation of the power of intercession come alive in her spirit, and it has changed this family for the glory of the Lord. She began to *pray the Word*, not just pray words.

> *But if our gospel be hid, it is hid to them that are lost: In whom the god of this world hath blinded the minds of them which believe not, lest the light of the glorious gospel of Christ, who is the image of God, should shine unto them* (II Corinthians 4:3-4).

Do you have lost loved ones? Pray their minds be un-blinded so they can hear, see and receive the truth of Jesus Christ into their hearts. I have personally seen this happen time after time as people begin to learn who they are in Jesus and who He is in them. There is no greater power in the universe today than the power of the children of God going to battle through prayer.

The Lord promises us in Proverbs 11:21 that "the seed of the righteous *shall be delivered.*" What makes us righteous? *The blood of Jesus*. We can stand on the promise of God, pray the Word and see our seed brought into the Kingdom of Christ! Hallelujah!

We have four grandchildren and they *just believe,*

because they have seen the Lord move in such mighty ways since they were born. The Lord told me He gave me grandchildren to keep me balanced. I have a tendency to get off with the Lord and forget the everyday things of life. When the kids come to visit, that can't happen.

Our grandchildren are the sixth generation of born-again, Spirit-filled believers on my mother's side of the family. Now *that's* blessed seed!

I *expect* the blessing of the Lord on my children and grandchildren because I have prayed the promises of God over them since they were born.

If you missed out on that when you were young, don't fret. The Lord is more than able to take your mistakes and turn them into miracles if you will let Him. Start today to pray the Word of God for their lives. Get into the presence of the Lord and get a battle plan to invade the enemy's camp and take back all that has been stolen because of ignorance or disobedience unto the Lord.

Remember what the Word says: If our Gospel is hidden, it is hidden to them that are lost. *Why?* Because the god of this world has blinded them so they can't see the light of Jesus Christ (II Corinthians 4:3-4). Unbind the minds—that's a missile of intercession we need to use against the enemy. The Lord told me what the Patriot missile was to bringing down the Scud missiles in Iraq, so is our intercession to the kingdom of God.

According to Webster, a patriot is one who loves and zealously protects or defends his country. *This world is not my home anymore!* I want to be a part of that air attack on the enemy. I want to prepare for that ground war! I want to go in and possess the land, take back what the enemy has stolen and occupy until Jesus comes.

Praise and worship will bring personal victory. Intercession will bring victory to the Body, the Bride of Christ. It will purify, cleanse, convict of sin, set apart, heal, deliver and set the captives free. The end result will be to glorify and magnify the Father through Jesus, the Son, by the power of the Holy Spirit and the authority of the shed Blood of the Lamb.

Who are the intercessors? The front line soldiers, storming the gates, protecting the land and turning back the enemy—in full battle array, marching to the beat of the sounds of victory!

And His wife has made herself ready!

Chapter 5

Needed: Laborers for the Harvest

Pray ye therefore the Lord of the harvest (Matthew 9:38).

. . . The harvest truly is great, but the laborers are few: pray ye therefore the Lord of the harvest, that He would send forth laborers into His harvest (Luke 10:2).

Praise and worship will bring personal victory and move us into a right relationship with the Lord. That's the key that unlocks the door.

Intercession will bring victory to the Body of Christ. What the Patriot was to the Iraqi scuds, so is our intercession to the kingdom of God. Intercession is the air attack that prepares us for ground war. . . the power that brings results to the Body of Christ.

It is time for the Bride of Christ to *put on her combat boots and begin to march into the enemy's camp*!

21

And when He was demanded of the Pharisees, when the kingdom of God should come, He answered them and said, The kingdom of God cometh not with observation: Neither shall they say, Lo here! Or, Lo there! For, behold, the kingdom of God is within you (Luke 17:20-21).

What was Jesus saying to these religious people? He said the kingdom of God is not an outward manifestation of something that can be seen approaching. It is an inward experience which will manifest itself *through* the one who has experienced the indwelling of the glory of God. He will make Himself known *through His people*. The world can't see it coming in, but the world *should* see it going out.

Be glad then, ye children of Zion, and rejoice in the Lord your God: for He hath given you the former rain moderately, and He will cause to come down for you the rain, the former rain, and the latter rain in the first month. And the floors shall be full of wheat, and the vats shall overflow with wine and oil. And I will restore to you the years that the locust hath eaten, the cankerworm, and the caterpillar, and the palmerworm, my great army which I sent among you (Joel 2:23-25, emphasis added).

Notice something here: This great army was sent *by the Lord* to devour.

> *Behold, the days come, saith the Lord God, that I will send a famine in the land, not a famine of bread, nor a thirst for water, but of hearing the words of the Lord* (Amos 8:11).

I heard the story of a pastor who was called to the hospital to minister to a dying man. He asked this man if he could pray with him for the forgiveness of sin that he might accept the Lord as his Savior. This man, with his dying breath said, "I don't know, nor do I have any *desire* to know your Jesus." He stepped out into eternity. . . lost.

How many babies have to die? How many people have to die with AIDS? How many homosexuals can a nation have without the hand of God overthrowing it? There is no fear of God left in this nation! There is open sin on every corner of every large city in America. There is perversion and murder and devil worship and every blasphemy you can imagine going on *right now*, as you read this book!

You may say, "How can there be a famine of the Word with a church on every corner, Christian television and radio available to everyone, and Christian books and music in abundance? How can 100,000 people die every day in India of starvation when they have more cattle roaming around than we have in all of Texas?" *The people of India worship the cows!* They worship the cows just as the people that are dying spiritually worship their sin!

God has promised us, His Church, a time of restoration and power that will exceed all we've seen thus far. That time is at hand! That time is at the door! He's getting ready to send forth His anointed ones into the harvest field with His kingdom power and authority to set the captives free. When Jesus says that the kingdom of God is within you, we need to realize the magnitude of this statement. When Jesus uses illustrations from the visible world to describe the kingdom of God (the kingdom of God is like unto), He is not using the real to depict the unreal; He is using the visible reality to depict *invisible reality*.

When He prays, "Thy kingdom come, Thy will be done in earth, as it is in heaven" (Matthew 6:10), He is actually praying that the invisible things of the heavenly realm should *control* and *manifest* themselves through the visible things of the earthly realm.

For the kingdom of God is not in word, but in power (I Corinthians 4:20).

Paul says, "*in demonstration of power and Spirit.*" Realizing our power in spiritual warfare is the power and might of the kingdom of God, we should not be surprised at the extent of that power. The first disciples were surprised (Luke 10:17-20). They returned saying, ". . . Lord, even the devils are subject unto us through Thy name."

Jesus, however, was not astonished (v.18). He saw

Satan fall as lightning from heaven. He knew the extent of the power of the kingdom. He knew that kingdom power had crushed the head of the enemy. When Satan was flung from heaven (his place of authority in God's kingdom), his power was broken. All power now belonged to the Son of Man and to whomever He would give it.

> *Behold, I give unto you Power to tread on serpents and scorpions, and over* all *the power of the enemy: and nothing shall by any means hurt you* (Luke 10:19, emphasis added).

James 1:22 tells us we are to be doers of the Word. If we are not *doers*, we are deceiving ourselves.

The Church is weak today because it is full of unbelievers. Not in the sense that they don't believe in Jesus as their Savior, but unbelievers in the sense they do not accept what God reveals to them in the Word concerning their power, authority and resources with which He has equipped them for spiritual warfare. *They have believer's credentials, but functionally they are unbelievers.*

> *The natural man can not receive the things of God; they are spiritual and therefore, must be discerned spiritually* (I Corinthians 2:9-16).

But We Have the Mind of Christ!

God will reveal things to us and instruct us. A

missionary was working in a new area in the mountains of Brazil and Uruguay in South America. He was witnessing in a village situated directly on the border of the two nations. In fact, the border ran down the middle of Main Street. He was distributing tracts during a shopping day when he noticed something quite unusual. On the Uruguayan side of the street, no one would accept his Gospel tracts. But on the Brazilian side, everyone accepted the tracts graciously and were open to hearing his testimony concerning his faith in Christ. He moved back and forth across the street with the same bewildering results.

Then he noticed a woman who had refused his tract on the Uruguayan side of the street crossing to the Brazilian side. He followed her and offered again the Gospel tract; this time she accepted it gratefully. He was able to witness to her about the Lord.

The missionary realized something very strange was going on. He began checking with other missionaries and believers in that particular part of Brazil. He discovered there was a group of Christians who had entered into spiritual warfare and were involved in intercessory prayer. They had literally taken authority over and bound the prince in that area of Brazil. Whenever the Gospel was preached there, tremendous revival was occurring. But, the awesome realization that shook the missionary was the fact that the revival ended at the geographical boundary; the stronghold over the area of Brazil ended at the border—*in the center of Main Street!*

It is interesting to note that when Jesus went into the wilderness to be tested, He went full of the Holy Ghost. But when He came out, He was full of power (Luke 4:14).

There is an obvious difference between being filled with the Spirit and moving in the power of the Spirit. This difference of spiritual maturity is the difference between having the potential of the Spirit's Power and actually using the power of the Word of God to defeat Satan. *This is spiritual warfare.* By learning about the power of the Word of God to overcome the devil, and using the Word of God as a great weapon, we move into an area of faith where the power of the Holy Spirit begins to move in our lives. We must be equipped with a knowledge and understanding of its total authority.

There is no place in the Word of God that says Satan ever defeated anyone. *He can only deceive*! When we believe his deception, then we bring defeat upon ourselves because we don't believe God's Word. We accept the evil report and believe the giants are bigger than the promise of God. That is when we suffer defeat. We must realize Satan is a *defeated enemy*. Jesus defeated him at Calvary and that victory has been given to us!

Whose Report Will We Believe?

And this is the confidence that we have in Him, that, if we ask any thing according to His will, He heareth us; And if we know that He hear us,

*whatsoever we ask, we know that we have the pe-
titions that we desired of Him* (I John 5:14-15).

We know the power of the God we serve!

Chapter 6

Free to Be

And ye shall know the truth, and the truth shall make you free (John 8:32).

It is not just truth that makes a person free, it is knowing truth that brings the freedom. Truth has always been, but unless you have the knowledge of that truth, you will continue to walk in darkness.

What is truth? Webster says that truth is "conformity with the facts or with reality." Jesus said in John 14:6, "I am the way, the truth, and the life. . . . "

The Greek word in these particular passages for "truth" is *aletheia*, which means, "not concealing or all revealing." The Greek word for "the way" is *hodos* and means, "the route to or means of getting to a destination." The word for "life" is transposed from several different words and actually means "vitality" or "essence of being." So, John 14:6 is saying Jesus is the means of our getting to our destination, and He is the reality that gives to us our vitality, or very essence of being. What a statement!

The Lord tells us in Colossians 2:10 that we are complete in Him—body, soul and spirit. That's how He wants us to be: complete.

Now, let's take a look at the word "free." We all think we know what it means. The Greek word is *el'euther'oo* and means "to exempt from mortal liability; no longer a slave to" or "at liberty." As Christians we all want to be free from sin. The question is: do we really understand what Jesus wants to accomplish in us through His work of the cross?

Iniquity: Unrighteousness Within That Causes Us to Sin

Simply put, sin is breaking the laws of God. This is what God calls transgressions.

> *If we confess our sins, He is faithful and just to forgive us our sins, and to cleanse us from all unrighteousness* (I John 1:9).

> *But He was wounded for our transgressions* [sin], *He was bruised for our iniquities* [unrighteousness within that causes us to sin], *the chastisement of our peace was upon Him; and with His stripes we are healed* (Isaiah 53:5).

We are *complete in Him*; physically, spiritually, mentally and emotionally.

For all have sinned, and come short of the Glory of God (Romans 3:23).

So, why are we even here? Why was I ever born?

Even every one that is called by My name; for I have created him for My glory, *I have formed him; yea, I have made him* (Isaiah 43:7, emphasis added).

We were created to bring glory to the Father in all we say and do. Yet we all have sinned and come short of the glory of God. We have all missed the mark. That is why the Lord Jesus Christ had to come to earth to redeem us from our fallen nature. However, He doesn't just want to redeem us from sin, but from *all unrighteousness.*

Iniquity—that unrighteousness within that causes us to sin.

Christians tend to deal with the sin in their life, but the iniquity is still there and they wonder why they go from one state of yielding to temptation to another. Most Christians don't even realize there is a difference between sin and iniquity. They just put it all in the same bucket and never endeavor to get to the root of the sin that *so easily besets them.*

Here's an example I heard about. A Christian brother was having a real problem with the sin of pornography. He realized this was a problem, so he went to the church leadership for the needed deliverance. He had counseling and thought the problem was taken care of. A year later, however, this same man was in the midst of an adulterous affair. The ministers couldn't understand why. The sin of pornography had been taken care of and through the power of the blood of Jesus Christ that was his as a child of God, he overcame that particular sin. However, the root of iniquity was still there, and since it was an iniquity of sexual perversion, adultery was simply the next manifestation of that iniquity. The unrighteousness within him that caused him to sin *was still there* in the darkness of the soul that had not yet been touched with the light of Christ. Because of that fact, the freedom or *the exemption from mortal liability* was not there.

Jesus wants to cleanse us from all unrighteousness that causes us to sin. You shall know the truth, and the truth shall make you free. Remember, it's not the truth that makes us free, it's *knowing* the truth that brings the freedom.

> *My people are destroyed for lack of knowledge: because thou hast rejected knowledge, I will also reject thee, that thou shalt be no priest to Me: seeing thou hast forgotten the law of thy God, I will also forget thy children* (Hosea 4:6).

Because *you have rejected*—that makes it a "choice" situation. Rejected what? Rejected *knowledge,* which is the revelation of truth. He then says, "I will also forget thy children."

Visiting the iniquity of the fathers on the children unto the third and fourth generation of them that hate God, passing that iniquity, that unrighteousness within, that causes us to sin unto the third and fourth generation of our children! In some instances, it was passed down to the tenth generation (Deuteronomy 23).

"Oh, but we don't hate God! That isn't talking about us!" Jesus said, "If you love Me, you will keep My commandments." *Obey His Word!* Some of you may be saying, "Oh, but that's Old Testament. It's talking about the priests saying, 'You will be no priest unto Me.'"

You are a chosen generation, a royal priesthood... (I Peter 2:9).

Oh, yes! That's talking about us.

Remember why you are here: to bring glory and honor to God in all that you say and do. If it doesn't bring glory to God, then you, in essence, have *missed the mark*, or sinned.

The Lord gave me a message on the true move of God's Spirit that He was trying to get across to His people. If it's just a work of the flesh or the soul, then it will bring glory and honor back upon the vessel (flesh) at the expense of God's glory. A good work can, in essence, become sin.

All we have to do to see examples of this is take a

look at the scandals that have rocked the Church in the last decade. Stealing God's glory resulted in sin that was rooted in iniquity to which the truth of Christ had not yet been revealed. Was that because God didn't want to reveal truth to certain dark areas of the soul? *Of course not!* It goes back to "because you have rejected knowledge."

What is the extent of the knowledge we must begin to deal with?

The Soul Ties

First of all, what is the soul? It is the *mind*, the *will* and the *emotions*. Remember, in Chapter Two we covered the points about the soul.

For this cause shall a man leave his father and mother, and shall be joined unto his wife, and they two shall be one flesh (Ephesians 5:31).

We need to realize that just because a relationship may end (divorce, death, separation or whatever the case may be), the fact that the *two have become one* has not changed. Not only do you become one in the flesh, but the "soul tie" has been made (with the mind, the will, the emotions) that reaches into the realm of the spirit. Verse 32 says,

This is a great mystery: but I speak concerning Christ and the church.

This is an allegory: the description of one thing under the image of another. Now turn to I Corinthians 6:16-20 and read the words of Paul.

Paul is saying, in essence, "What? Don't you realize that if you have sexual relations with a prostitute that you are as much one flesh as if you were man and wife?" Soul ties from sexual relationships are *not just flesh experiences*, but spiritual as well. The Lord said, "This is a mystery, I speak concerning Christ and the Church (Ephesians 5:32)." Jesus said we are to be one in Him as He and the Father are one. He's the Bridegroom and we are the Bride. The Word has to abide in us and us in the Word. What is the Word? In the beginning was the Word, and the Word became flesh and dwelt among men.

What does Satan want to destroy? *Your soul.*

What? Know ye not that your body is the temple of the Holy Ghost? Therefore, glorify God in your body and in your spirit which both belong to God.

If Satan can get you to become one with multiplied partners and form those fleshly soul ties, you will then have a fragmented soul. I have talked with many people who have had the same problems. They have gone from relationship to relationship and seem to end up in the same mess. They wonder why they continue to get partners that have the same shortcomings. They tend to subconsciously be drawn to the same type of person through the dark area of their soul that has affected their will and emotions because of the soul ties formed through the former relationships. A piece of their soul is still, in the realm of the spirit, connected to others. The Word of God says they become *one flesh.*

What is the answer? Recognize the truth and allow the Blood to renew your mind in Christ Jesus. Ask the Lord to break that soul tie which is still controlling a portion of your life. Ask Him to forgive your sin, cleanse you from the root of iniquity within and set you free. Just tell Him you want to know the truth and have the truth make you free in Him—and He will!

The next thing we need to look at is the *transference of spirits.* This can take place through sexual relationships as well. That's why every pagan religion has within its ceremonies some form of sexual ritual that takes place. Satan uses this as a means of taking up residence in people.

Let's look at another example of transference of spirits that takes place on a daily basis—*fear.* Fear produces worry, and worry is a sin or a falling short of the mark.

The thing which I greatly feared is come upon me (Job 3:25).

But the Lord says:

There is no fear in love; but perfect love casteth out fear: because fear hath torment. He that feareth is not made perfect in love (I John 4:18).

Perfect in love; complete in Him. Are you getting the picture? When we hear the word *tumor*, our fear speaks *cancer*. Worry grips our minds, and we react in our souls instead of responding in the spirit. That opens us up to the thing that we feared coming upon us.

> *Be careful for nothing [don't worry about any-thing]; but in every thing by prayer and supplica-tion with thanksgiving let your requests be made known unto God. And the peace of God, which pas-seth all understanding shall keep your hearts and minds through Christ Jesus* (Philippians 4:6-7).

The peace of God will bypass your natural mind and keep you in Him. You'll know the truth and the truth shall make you free. That peace of God which passes all under-standing is rightfully ours as children of the King.

Have you ever noticed that people tend to act like whomever they are around? The stronger spirit will over-ride the weaker one. *That's a transference of spirits!*

Now let's look at something else that can keep us from being free in Christ: *bloodline curses*, or the things that have been handed down from generation to genera-tion. This can be anything from disease to poverty. A good one to consider is being overweight. My mom was fat, my grandma was fat, my aunts are all fat, so I'm just destined to be fat! That's just my lot in life. *Oh, no it's not!* Break that curse that's been handed down from gen-eration to generation.

What happens when we go to the doctor for the first time? He asks us to list our family history. Who has heart disease, diabetes, how many in your family have died of cancer. . . ?

The doctor is saying, "List for me all the *bloodline curses* that have been handed down from one generation to the next so I know what to look for in you!" *Let the blood of Jesus break those bloodline curses once and for all!*

He Already Paid the Price!

These are just highlights of some hidden truths that need the light of Jesus Christ shed on them:

How can we get to that place of victory?
How can we know the truth and be made free?
How can we keep the healings and the victories after we receive them?

Jesus wants you to know you are free to be all He created you to be. He has already done all that needs to be done for us to walk in that victory.

Chapter 7

Walking in Victory

But thanks be to God, which giveth us the victory through our Lord Jesus Christ (I Corinthians 15:57).

What must we do to attain that victory? First of all, we must *recognize the battle of the mind, that doorway to the soul, and be renewed, or made new, in the* spirit *of our mind* (Ephesians 4:23, emphasis added).

Notice that it is in the *spirit* of our mind, not in the flesh of our mind. We can take that sin under control, but if the iniquity is laying dormant in the spirit of our mind, we will continue to battle with the same type failures and frustrations and wonder *why*, when we are a born-again Christian. In Matthew 3:10, John the Baptist said you have to put the ax to the *root* of the tree. Any tree that does not bring forth good fruit needs to be cut down.

I beseech you therefore, brethren, by the mercies

> *of God, that ye present your bodies a living sacri-*
> *fice, holy, acceptable unto God, which is your rea-*
> *sonable service. And be not conformed to this*
> *world: but be ye transformed by the* renewing of
> your mind, *that ye may prove what is that good,*
> *and acceptable, and perfect, will of God* (Romans
> 12:1-2, emphasis added).

Paul is talking to the brothers in the church. He goes
on to tell them that this request is only a *reasonable ser-*
vice. That tells me it *can* be done.

You may be walking in that *good will* of God today.
You're a Christian, but there is no victory in your life.
You aren't experiencing any growth. You don't have the
joy of the Holy Ghost. Then there are the ones who are
walking in that *acceptable will* of the Lord. These are the
ones who are doing good works and are striving to be
good enough to please the Lord. They go from one seminar to another, from one revival to another, from one
work to another. They are walking in His *permissive will*.
If it's a drawing of the Spirit that is taking you from place
to place, you will produce fruit that remains. If it's just a
good work of the flesh, you will burn out long before
Jesus comes. You can be busy doing good works and miss
God's work if you are not totally led by His Spirit.

There is the *perfect will of the Father* which brings
victory in the midst of the storm and *power* to overcome
the works of the flesh. You will know that whatever
comes your way, Jesus is still Lord of all. Job gone? *Jesus*

is Lord! Illness strikes? *Jesus is Lord!* Banks go under? *Jesus is* still *Lord!*

> *Therefore if any man be in Christ, he is a new creature: old things are passed away; behold, all things are become new* (II Corinthians 5:17).

The Key: Be in Christ

> *If ye abide in Me, and My words abide in you, ye shall ask what ye will, and it shall be done unto you. Herein is My Father glorified, that ye bear much fruit; so shall ye be My disciples* (John 15:7-8).

Why are we here? Why were we born? *To bring glory to the Father!* Now, how can we keep the victory? We must *know our weapons*!

> *For the weapons of our warfare are not carnal, but mighty through God to the pulling down of strong holds; Casting down imaginations, and every high thing that exalteth itself against the knowledge of God, and bringing into captivity every thought to the obedience of Christ* (II Corinthians 10:4-5).

That is our job! God has done His part—now it is up to us to do ours. Remember: ". . . because thou hast rejected knowledge. . ." (Hosea 4:6).

If we obey all these commands, what will be the results?

1. You will think differently.

Your soul will no longer be tormented with the iniquity that was rooted in ignorance of truth.

2. You will feel different.

Though we do not base our life on feelings, when you are motivated, have more freedom, have newfound joy and so forth, there is a growth process that takes place. Growing produces *feelings*. In the natural realm, it can be compared to puberty. So it is in the realm of the spiritual growth.

3. You will act differently.

Luke 3:8 says, "Bring forth therefore fruits worthy of repentance. . . " Acts 26:20 states ". . . do works meet for repentance. . . " Because you are changing and growing in the Lord, your *life* will be different. If there is not a change in your actions, you simply have a head knowledge of who Jesus is. You need to receive a heart knowledge that will produce a change in your life.

4. You will receive differently.

If you have a problem receiving blessings from the Lord, especially if He chooses what you consider to be the wrong person to bless you, then you need to grow in the grace and knowledge of the Lord Jesus Christ.

His plan for His children is to be blessed. He tells us in Deuteronomy 28 that we will be blessed if we obey and cursed if we don't. The choice is ours. It's meat for the children's table and bread for the saints of God.

Have you been born again? Have you been filled with His Spirit? Are there buried emotions from refusing to acknowledge truth that has you bound? Do you have anger, bitterness, unforgiveness, fear, hopelessness, worry, anxiety or any of the works of the flesh that are keeping you in bondage? There are multitudes of women who have an intense hatred for men because they were molested as a child or sexually abused as a young girl.

Do soul ties, bloodline curses, sexual sins, feelings of abandonment, torment from an abortion, drugs or alcohol have a hold on you? Allow the Spirit of Christ to reveal to you what is needed to bring about your freedom. The choice is yours; the choice is mine. We must *choose* to take up our bed and walk. We must *choose* to walk in the light and obedience to His Word.

The choice is ours! *We are free in Jesus to walk in total victory!* Jesus came to bring freedom to the captives. He died to save, deliver and heal His children. Some of us are in need of *deliverance* from the powers of darkness. Jesus paid the price so that could be done. Acknowledge His truth and we will be made free in Christ Jesus, our Lord, providing we accept and walk in what He died to give us.

Chapter 8

The Power to Bind and Loose

Whatsoever thou shalt bind on earth shall be bound in heaven (Matthew 16:19).

The Spirit of the Lord God is upon me; because the Lord hath anointed me to preach good tidings unto the meek; He hath sent me to bind up the brokenhearted, to proclaim liberty to the captives, and the opening of the prison to them that are bound (Isaiah 61:1).

Jesus said:

The Spirit of the Lord is upon Me, because He hath anointed Me to preach the gospel to the poor; He hath sent Me to heal the brokenhearted, to preach deliverance to the captives, and recovering of sight to the blind, to set at liberty them that are bruised (Luke 4:18).

According to the Word, Jesus holds in His hands at least three keys. We need to understand that keys denote authority and responsibility.

I am He that liveth and was dead; and, behold, I am alive forever more, Amen; and have the keys of death and hell (Revelation 1:18).

So, we know from this Scripture that Jesus holds the keys of death and hell. What's another key He holds?

And the key of the house of David will I lay upon His shoulder; so that He shall open, and none shall shut; and He shall shut, and none shall open (Isaiah 22:22).

Revelation 3:7 says basically the same thing.

Another key then is the *key of David*—the key of kingship. That's the ability to open and close doors that no man can open or close. Just a few examples to help you understand the magnitude of this:

The Door of Understanding

Withal praying also for us, that God would open unto us a door of utterance, to speak the mystery of Christ, for which I am also in bonds: That I may make it manifest, as I ought to speak. (Colossians 4:3-4).

Only the Spirit of the Lord can give us that understanding we need to put into action the truths of God and His Word.

The next door which only the Lord can open is:

The Door of Hearts

Even the mystery which hath been hid from ages and from generations, but now is made manifest to His saints (Colossians 1:26).

He answered and said unto them, Because it is given unto you to know the mysteries of the kingdom of heaven, but to them it is not given (Matthew 13:11).

These are ours to open with the key of knowledge.

We could go on and on with pertinent Scriptures for the key of knowledge, but we have also been given other keys.

And I will give unto thee the keys of the kingdom of heaven: and whatsoever thou shalt bind on earth shall be bound in heaven: and whatsoever thou shalt loose on earth shall be loosed in heaven (Matthew 16:19).

Notice, these keys are plural—more than one key. Why? Remember in Matthew we were told that it was given to us to understand the *mysteries of the kingdom of heaven.*

Have you heard the story about the platoon of Japanese soldiers who were stationed on a South Pacific island during World War II and had lost contact with the outside world? They had no way of communicating with anyone, and they did not know peace had been declared years before. They were fighting a war that was long over.

That's the way it is with many of God's children. They are fighting a war that was won long ago at Calvary by the blood of Jesus. He died and rose again to give us victory over *all* the power of the enemy. But, we must realize that the war has been won, and we just need to implement the weapons that are rightfully ours; and that includes the power to *bind and loose.* Part of the Lord's Prayer says:

> . . . *Thy kingdom come, Thy will be done in earth, as it is in heaven . . .* (Matthew 6:10).

Take note that Jesus put earth first. In Matthew 18:18 Jesus tells us:

> *Verily I say unto you, Whatsoever ye shall bind on earth shall be bound in heaven: and whatsoever ye shall loose on earth shall be loosed in heaven.*

Again, Jesus put earth first. It looks like earth governs

heaven. What God ordains as His Word must be carried out on earth in order for heaven to move. God wrote the Scriptures, we proclaim it on earth and finally, heaven moves to manifest the provision or promise of that Scripture.

We've been given the keys to the kingdom and with these keys the power to *bind and loose*. Matthew 16:18 tells us that the gates of hell cannot prevail against this power!

There's something important we need to understand here: God works with us on this! He says, "You bind, I bind; you loose, I loose." We have the power to move both things and people to accomplish the will of God. Now, let's take a closer look at what this actually means. In Matthew 6:14-15, the Lord says if we forgive others, then He will forgive us. If we don't forgive others, then God *can't forgive us*. God is bound by His Word. We, in essence, bind the hands of God. How?

Unforgiveness!

In Matthew 18:23-27 the Lord teaches on forgiveness with the parable of the debtor. In verse 27, the master of the servant forgave the debt and *loosed him*. We need to learn this principle of the kingdom: *Forgiveness will loose; unforgiveness will bind.*

Remember this! It is important! Forgiveness will loose and unforgiveness will bind. In order to comprehend this, we must look at John 20:21-23:

Then said Jesus to them again, Peace be unto you: as My Father hath sent Me, even so send I you. And when He had said this, He breathed on them, and saith unto them, Receive ye the Holy Ghost: Whose soever sins ye remit, they are remitted unto them; and whose soever sins ye retain, they are retained.

You may be saying "What has this got to do with anything?" Let's use the key of knowledge to unlock a mystery of the kingdom.

1. You must know you are being sent to accomplish God's plan (v. 21).

2. You must be filled with the Holy Ghost (v. 22). That's the only way you can fulfill number one and three.

3. Remit or forgive someone else's sin (v. 23).

Now, this does not mean I can be a go-between for a person and God. I cannot forgive their sins for them when they continue to walk in that sin. I can't be a priest to you and expect your confession of sin to me to set you free. Confession and repentance is not the same thing.

Repentance is necessary for the blood of Jesus to wash away your sins of commission. The Word of God says: ". . . go and sin no more. . . " Turn and go the other way. Have a change of heart and start walking toward a renewed mind in Christ. This is talking about our for-giving or remitting a sin that has been committed against us. Remember, forgiveness will loose and unforgiveness will bind. Whatsoever we bind on earth is bound in heaven, and whatsoever we loose on earth is loosed in heaven. It doesn't matter what has been committed against us, *we must remit that sin*, or we will not only bind ourselves, but will be the cause of the other person being bound as well.

I want to give you an example I heard about in a meeting I was in. The minister said he was preaching on the power of binding and loosing. After the service, a woman came up to him and asked him if it was possible to bind someone with sickness. He said he had to admit that he had never heard of that and wasn't sure exactly what she meant. She proceeded to tell him a story.

When she was just getting out of school and about to begin her adult life, her mother had a serious heart attack, and she had to change all her plans to take care of her. There was no choice in the matter, so her life was drasti-cally changed. Her mother recovered from the heart problem, but experienced one serious illness after another and had not even been able to prepare her daughter's breakfast one time in over 17 years.

This woman got saved, but continued to harbor re-sentment in her heart toward her mother for having ruined her life. She heard what the minister said that night and felt in her spirit the Lord was telling her she had bound her mother to a life of illness by her unforgiveness. The minister then told the woman to test this to see if it were true. She was to go home, wake her mother and tell her she forgave her for being ill and ruining her life. She did this and to her amazement, the very next morning, she awoke to the smell of bacon cooking. She had made the comment to the minister the night before that her mother had not even so much as cooked her breakfast in over 17 years. But there she was, in the kitchen, doing just that. She got out of bed, totally and completely healed.

Do you realize that our unforgiveness can bind a person to the very thing we hate? I heard this testimony and decided to put it to the test myself. I had no more than arrived home, when I got a call from a woman who was at her wits end with her husband. He had started using tobacco again after many years of freedom from the habit, and she was so angry she could hardly stand it. Her husband was a Christian who rebelled against the call of God.

His rebellion opened the door to compromise, and compromise leads to sin. But, the anger of the wife and *her unforgiveness was the very thing that was binding him to that sin*. I shared with her the story of the girl and her mother and told her to ask the Lord to help her *remit* her husband's sin. She had to be willing to forgive him for hurting her, as well as his Christian witness. She did just that, and her husband was turned totally around.

We must *activate* John 20:23 and remit the sins of others in our lives so we can know the truth of Matthew 6:15—God has forgiven us of our sins.

Once we know this truth in our spirit, we can then

begin to bind in a positive way. Proverbs 3:3 and 7:3 says we are to bind the truths of God about our neck and fingers and upon the tables of our heart. We can also bind the Word of God that fits our situation to the heart of the one involved. We can send the angels of the Lord to bind the Word of God around the neck of our loved ones as a necklace and upon their hands as rings on their fingers. To that woman with the husband problem, I told her to send the Word of God, which says that "rebellion is as the sin of witchcraft," and to break that sin off his life by loosing the sin (through forgiveness) and, in a positive way, binding around her husband the truth of the Word that says, "God is faithful to forgive our sins." She did. He did. *And then God did!*

Hebrews 1:14 tells us that the angels are ministering spirits sent forth to minister to those who are heirs of salvation. But the angels only respond to the Word of God. Send them with the Word. Find the Word that fits your situation to send forth and bind to that one who needs it: *health for sickness; prosperity for poverty; peace for strife; beauty for ashes; joy for mourning; and obedience for rebellion.*

But it has to happen on earth first! Can you see this? There's power in the statement that Jesus made right along with the binding and loosing Scripture when He said, "And the gates of hell shall not prevail. . . " (Matthew 16:18).

The Lord has promised that His Word will not return

to Him void, but will do the very thing He sends it forth to do (Isaiah 55:11).

He is bound by His Word! His Word will never fail. We have been given the keys to the kingdom. It is up to us to use them according to the Word. This is just more of God's strategy to help us live a life of overcoming power and victory. In Isaiah 45:11, the Lord says:

> *Thus saith the Lord, the Holy One of Israel, and his Maker, Ask Me things to come concerning My sons, and concerning the work of My hands command ye Me.*

We have the keys!

Chapter 9

That Appointed Time
for His Visitation

For the vision is yet for an appointed time, but at the end it shall speak, and not lie; though it tarry, wait for it; because it will surely come, it will not tarry (Habakkuk 2:3).

Habakkuk, a prophet of God, started his writing with a sob (1:2) and ended with a song (3:19). In these three short chapters, he experienced *transcendent prayer* and looked beyond the immediate to the promise of the God he served. He rose above the circumstances and prayed.

The answer to all our problems is the Lord Jesus Christ—and my becoming what He says I already am!

Remember, He said, ". . . Wait for it; it will surely come, it will not tarry (Habakkuk 2:3)."

We know the Lord said in Hosea 4:6 that His people are destroyed because of a lack of knowledge, so we need to endeavor to grasp ahold of the knowledge of the Lord.

Come, and let us return unto the Lord: for He hath torn and He will heal us; He hath smitten, and He will bind us up. After two days will He revive us: in the third day He will raise us up, and we shall live in His sight. Then shall we know, if we follow on to know the Lord: His going forth is prepared as the morning; and He shall come unto us as the rain, as the latter and former rain unto the earth (Hosea 6:1-3).

He shall come to us as the former rain and the latter rain.

In Luke 19, Jesus ". . . beheld the city and wept. . . ." In verse 42 it says that *in that day*, they missed the eternal peace which the man Jesus was offering them. He went on to say that not one stone would be left upon the other because they knew not the day of His visitation. He wasn't just talking about the stones of the literal temple. He was talking about the temple of God being made up of *living stones.*

He's the Rock—We're the Stones

Now, this was offered to the Jew first. He always goes to the Jew first.

I have yet many things to say unto you, but ye cannot bear them now. Howbeit when He, the Spirit of Truth, is come, He will guide you into all truth: for He shall not speak of Himself; but whatsoever He shall hear, that shall He speak: and he will shew you things to come. He shall glorify Me: for He shall receive of Mine, and shall shew it unto you. All things that the Father hath are Mine: therefore said I, that He shall take of Mine, and shall shew it unto you (John 16:12-15).

He had more for them but *they were not ready.* However, when the Spirit of truth is come, "Wait for it; for it will surely come. . . ." (Hosea 2:3); you will be able, like Habakkuk, to pray *transcendent prayers.*

Behold, the former things are come to pass, and new things do I declare: before they spring forth I tell you of them (Isaiah 42:9).

Surely the Lord God will do nothing, but He revealeth His secret unto His servants the prophets (Amos 3:7).

Remember ye not the former things, neither consider the things of old. Behold, I will do a new thing; NOW it shall spring forth; shall ye not know it? *I will even make a way in the wilderness, and rivers in the desert* (Isaiah 43:18- 19, emphasis added).

Hear what the Lord is saying to His people. There is

an appointed time for His visitation, and He is preparing His people for that time! He is busy getting us prepared for the wedding and prepared for the war!

That's the Bride Wearing Combat Boots

Look again at Hosea 6:1-3:

Come, and let us return unto the Lord: for He hath torn and He will heal us: He hath smitten, and He will bind us up. After two days will He revive us: in the third day He will raise us up, and we shall live in His sight. Then shall we know, if we follow on to know the Lord: His going forth is prepared as the morning: and He shall come unto us as the rain, as the latter and former rain unto the earth.

II Peter 3:8 tells us that a day is with the Lord as a thousand years, and a thousand years as one day. He tells us to *not to be ignorant of that one thing.*

If you think I am being repetitious, it's because I'm doing it for a purpose. I want you to hear what the Lord is saying. I declare that this is *that day* the Lord is talking about! I believe we are at the end of day two, going into day three. *The appointed time for His visitation; the time of resurrection, restoration and revelation!*

Shall ye not know it? Then shall we know, if we

follow on to know the Lord. That I may know Him, *and the power of His resurrection, and the fellowship of His sufferings, being made conformable unto His death* (Philippians 3:10, emphasis added).

The devil is trying to kill you and the Lord is trying to kill you! Which death do you want?

My heart aches for those who will miss the time of His visitation because of their lack of hunger for the things of God. He is coming for a people *whether we are ready or not.* Can you hear the Lord shouting from the heavens: "Here I come, ready or not"?

Who is He coming for?

Chapter 10

Kings and Priests Unto the Lord

*And hath made us kings and priests unto God and His Father (*Revelation 1:6).

The Lord says in Revelation 1:6 that He has made us kings and priests unto Him. Then in I Peter 2:9, He tells us we are a royal priesthood, a peculiar people. You may be thinking He is talking about the children of Israel, the seed of Abraham, but look at Galatians 3:29 and you will find that, if we are *Christ's*, then we are Abraham's seed and heirs according to the promise *because of the blood of Jesus*!

He became our High Priest and our blood sacrifice all in one in order that we may become a *royal priesthood*. We are now Abraham's seed. What did the priests in the Old Testament do? They took the blood of the sacrifice and once a year entered into the Holy of Holies to redeem the people from their sins. But, we are told to enter boldly into the throne room of grace as His redeemed children (Hebrews 4:16).

In the tabernacle of Moses, there were three places for the people. (Now remember, the Old Testament is a type and shadow of the New Testament in Christ.)

The first place was the *Outer Court*. We can liken this to having Jesus as our Savior, the forgiver of our sins. All the people could go here. It is still the same today. All can enter into the outer court.

The second place was the *Inner Court* or the *Holy Place*. We liken this to Jesus, our Christ, or the anointing through the Holy Spirit. To enter into the Holy Place, you must have the anointing of the Holy Spirit. Only the priesthood could enter in here. The first priests were Aaron and Aaron's sons: Nadab, Abihu, Eleazar and Ithamar (Exodus 28:1). This also represents the five-fold ministry.

The third place was the *Most Holy Place* or the *Holy of Holies*. Only the High Priest could enter into the Most Holy Place. In this place, *Jesus Is Lord*. In this place, you truly realize you are not your own anymore. You have been bought with a price!

In the Holy of Holies, the Mercy Seat of the Lord rested between the cherubim which was upon the Ark of the Covenant. It was here that His Presence was made known and the *Almighty God communed with the High Priest* (Exodus 25:22). (Remember, all things in the Old Testament are a type and shadow of that new and better covenant.)

The only way to get to the Most Holy Place was to go through the door. John 10:9 tells us Jesus is our door.

After entering the door, you must wash in the laver and be regenerated by the washing of the water by the Word, which is found in Ephesians 5:26 and Titus 3:5. Then you must pass the altar of incense, which represents praise and worship. We find this in John 4:23 and Revelation 8:4.

Let my prayer be set forth before Thee as incense; and the lifting up of my hands as the evening sacrifice (Psalm 141:2).

The word "prayer" in this passage means "intercession, petition or hymn." It is when we get to the place of true praise and worship that we, as priests of the Most High God, can enter into the Holy of Holies or the Most Holy Place. When we do that, it is then that we will hear Him say, ". . . and there I will meet with thee, and I will commune with thee from above the mercy seat. . . " (Exodus 25:22). In this place, we, as kings and priests, know Him as Jesus Christ Our Lord! As kings and priests, we are to minister *for* Him and *unto* Him.

There are many things which can hinder this call of God on our life. We have the tendency to just consider as hindrances what we can see with the naked eye as blatant sin. But, what does God say are the hindrances to the priesthood or your ministry unto others? I want to review Leviticus 21:16-24 and remind you of the *type and shadow* of the Old and New Testaments.

First, before we consider the so-called blemishes that stop a priest from entering into the Most Holy Place, let's see exactly what he is forbidden to do.

. . . He shall not come nigh to offer the bread of his God (v. 21b).

Verse 22 tells us he can eat it himself, but he can't give it to others to eat.

What or who is the bread? John 6:31-35 tells us *Jesus is the bread*. Remember, we are talking about being priests unto the Lord, not necessarily offices of ministry. We are all called to come to the Holy of Holies.

Go ye into all the world . . . (Mark 16:15).
These signs shall follow them that believe . . . (Mark 16:17).

Now, let's look at the blemishes which were preventative to serving the bread to others.

1. Blind — No vision

Where there is no vision, the people perish; but he that keepeth the law, happy is he (Proverbs 29:18).

If you are without vision, you are the same as blind and can't offer the bread to others, though you, yourself, may freely eat.

2. Lame — Can't go forward
In Acts 3:2 we have the story of the man who was

lame from his mother's womb. He had to be taken wherever he was going, and there he had to stay. The same is true of the spiritually lame. They can't go forward. If that is true of you, then you can eat of the bread, but you can't feed others.

3. Flat Nose — No discernment

They have ears, but they hear not: noses, have they, but they smell not (Psalm 115:6).

The Lord says in this last day, the army of the Lord, the priest and kings will need to have a nose to smell. They must be able to discern between the true and false, between the true light and the angel of light, between the real and the counterfeit of the enemy.

4. Superfluous — Having excess members (More of me than there should be!)

John the Baptist said he had to decrease in order for Jesus to increase (John 3:30). We must put to death the flesh! If we don't, we will not be able to feed others the bread.

5. Broken-Footed — Unbalanced

This is not the same thing as being lame. If you are broken-footed, you can walk, but you are *unbalanced*. Paul said in Acts 20:27:

For I have not shunned to declare unto you all the counsel of God.

He's saying, "I have given you a balance of truth." Without that, you may eat, but you will never effectively feed others as a priest unto the Lord.

6. Broken-Handed — the works of your hands
This speaks of the works of your hands. You have to be willing to *do something.* Jesus kept saying to the churches in the book of Revelation that He knew their works and he would "judge[d] every man according to their works (Revelation 20:13b)."

7. Crookbacked — walks all bent over
In the realm of the spirit, this says they have nothing but an earthly vision. This can be related to the seed that was sown among the thorns in Matthew 13:22:

He also that received seed among the thorns is he that heareth the Word; and the care of this world, and the deceitfulness of riches, choke the Word, and he becometh unfruitful.

8. Dwarf — Stunted Growth
Never mature to the full stature of Christ.

I have fed you with milk and not with meat: for hitherto ye were not able to bear it, neither yet now are ye able. For ye are yet carnal: for whereas there is among you envying, and strife, and divisions, are ye not yet carnal, and walk as men? (I Corinthians 3:2-3).

Or, we could say, *walk as dwarfs.* Are you still at the same place in the Lord as you were a year ago, a month ago, or even last week? If so, you may be a *spiritual dwarf* and therefore not chosen by the Lord to be a priest unto Him.

9. Blemish in Eye — Blurred vision

Mark 8:22-25 tells us of a blind man on whom Jesus laid hands and then asked him how he could see. The man said he saw men walking as trees. *He had blurred vision.* This was not good enough. The Lord touched him again and he *saw every man clearly.* In order to be a priest and offer the bread to others, we must see men clearly as the Lord would have us to; knowing no man after the flesh, but by the Spirit of God (II Corinthians 5:16).

10. Scurvy — Diseased by the wrong diet

You are what you eat. Proverbs 13:2 states:

A man shall eat good by the fruit of his mouth: but the soul of the transgressors shall eat violence.

And die with spiritual scurvy!

11. Scabbed — Hard, crusty spots
Unforgiveness, anger and bitterness are a few of these scabbed areas. Jesus said:

> *But if ye do not forgive, neither will your Father which is in heaven forgive your trespasses* (Mark 11:26).

If you are spiritually scabbed, you cannot enter into the Holy of Holies as a priest or offer the bread to others.

12. Broken Stones — reproductiveness
A man with broken stones cannot bear fruit! Our reproductiveness is in Jesus!! If we do not stay connected to Him, we will be as a man with broken stones.

Jesus tells us all about being reproductive and bearing fruit unto the Lord in John 15:1-8: ". . .So shall ye be my disciples. . . so shall ye be kings and priests unto me!"

Hear what the Spirit of the Lord is saying to them that are being called into this preparation of warfare! *What is hindering your priesthood? What is stopping you from offering the bread of life unto others? What is standing in the way of your becoming all that He says you can be?*

There are those who may never see you as a king or priest unto the Lord. They just do not have the understanding of that principle or they are not walking in that revelation. But, are you looked upon as a strength in a time of trouble for them? Can they hear your name and feel in their hearts that you are someone they can count on to be a stable force in their life if need be? Can they consider you to be a nail in a sure place?

Chapter 11

A Nail in a Sure Place

And I will fasten him as a nail in a sure place; and he shall be for a glorious throne to his father's house. And they shall hang upon him all the glory of his father's house (Isaiah 22:23-24).

I read a book, *A Nail in a Sure Place* written by Margaret Jensen. She said, "We are all nails, all there for someone to hang onto."

As I pondered this thought, I realized the powerful truth of this statement and had to wonder how many are trying to be a nail for someone to hang onto without having the *surety of the place*. I believe God fastens or *nails* people in our lives to help fulfill His plan of purpose for us. Sometimes we may not like *who* He has nailed us to, but, if we can only realize that God sees the end from the beginning, then we can not only appreciate more the nails He's given us, but also *become* one for someone else to hold on to when they fall down the mountain of life.

In mountain climbing, the leader of the group pounds

A Nail in a Sure Place

iron pegs into the mountain as hand grips for the others to hold onto. We need to hear what the Lord is saying to us with this—*eternal truths never change*! They are the iron pegs for us to hold on to as He fastens us as nails in a sure place. You may be the only nail in your family, on your job, in your community, but God will make a way for you to hang in there.

We sometimes feel like anything *but* that nail in a sure place, but if we hold on to the iron pegs of God's eternal truths, we will not come loose and fall.

The first eternal truth we must hold on to is: ***In the beginning, God***. We must believe He is the beginning and the end. If we have that surety, then we can know that He has a plan for the "in between." Jesus is the way! The greatest power in our lives is the atonement of Jesus—*at-one-ment* (one with God). It is called *redemption*!

Oswald Chambers said, "The Holy Spirit is deity in proceeding power, who applies the atonement to our experience, and works in us the nature of Christ." That is truly putting Romans 8:28 in a nutshell:

And we know that all things work together for good to them that love God, to them who are the called according to His purpose.

The second iron peg is ***the Word of God***.

For the Word of God is quick and powerful, and sharper than any two-edged sword, piercing even to the dividing asunder of soul and spirit, and of the joints and marrow, and is a discerner of the thoughts and intents of the heart (Hebrews 4:12).

For ever, Oh Lord, Thy Word is settled in heaven (Psalm 119:89).

For God so loved the world, that He gave His only begotten Son, that whosoever believeth in Him should not perish, but have everlasting life (John 3:16).

The Word of God is quick and powerful. How long is His Word settled in heaven? Forever! Do we really realize what is being said here? *Do we really understand that the Creator of the Universe is speaking?* Can we possibly comprehend that He is talking to us? How He must mourn at times at the lack of understanding of His children!

This takes us right to our third iron peg, ***the promises of God***. Just to name a few:

. . . *Lo, I am with you always* (Matthew 28:20).

. . . *I will never leave thee, nor forsake thee* (Hebrews 13:5).

If ye abide in Me, and My words abide in you, ye

shall ask what ye will, and it shall be done unto you (John 15:7).

. . . Be of good cheer; I have overcome the world (John 16:33).

God's Word is full of promises. But then comes the battle to *believe* those promises. The testing of our faith— obedience to God's Word—and these iron pegs or *eternal truths* will help make us to be a nail in a sure place for someone who is falling.

There are many other things in life that can be a nail in a sure place:

1. Laughter

A merry heart doeth good like a medicine (Proverbs 17:22).

2. Friends

A man that hath friends must shew himself friendly: and there is a friend that sticketh closer than a brother (Proverbs 18:24).

3. Memories

I will remember the works of the Lord; surely I will remember Thy wonders of old (Psalm 77:11).

When I was growing up, I saw many wonders of the Lord in my Grandfather's church. I remember seeing my Great Uncle Jimmy, after six years of total blindness, having his eyes opened by the hand of God during the worship service. I remember the crutches, the dark glasses, the canes and other paraphernalia of afflictions that were strung across the front of the altar. Because of this nail in a sure place, I never wondered if God loved me or if He would be there when I called upon His Name. I *knew* if I was doing my part, He would surely do His. This has kept me many times when I felt as though I were falling down the side of the mountain.

You know who I've found to be a "nail in a sure place" in my life? My grandchildren!

The Lord told me one time that He gave me grandchildren for my balance. My children just *thought* it was their idea to have kids. I remember Tara Lynn at the age of 15 months sitting on my lap in the car as we were on our way to a service. The window was down, and the wind was blowing in our faces. She couldn't get over the fact that she could feel the wind but couldn't see it. I told her to try to catch the wind so we could see it. She tried and tried to catch the wind because Grandma told her to. That gave me a perfect illustration for the service that night for those who had a difficult time believing for the baptism in the Holy Spirit.

Another time we were coming home from service and the roads were icy. There was a car that had slid off the road, and a policeman was there with his cruiser to help them. As we passed the police car, Tara said, "Grandma, pray for the policeman." I said, "It's okay, honey. He's not hurt. He's just there to help the people that slid off the road." A few seconds later, Bob asked me, "What's Tara doing?" I looked at her and she was mumbling right along. I said, "Tara, what are you doing?" She looked at me as only a two-year-old could and said, "Well, Grandma, *somebody* around here has to pray for that policeman." A "nail in a sure place!"

I remember Laura Beth after she had tubes put in her ears. I asked her if she could hear better now that she had her tubes. She said, "I sure can. Daddy sounds like God!" Just another "nail in a sure place!"

Then there's the weekend that Tiffany stayed with us. I tried to plan a fun time for her—one she would remember. We went to the mall and did some dollar store shopping, ate pizza, went to see the latest kid's movie that was out and then went swimming. When her Mom picked her up and asked her what fun things she had done at Mammy's, Tiffany excitedly told her she read two whole chapters of the book of Esther and even said, "Mor-din'-a-cad'-dee-iiiii." That was Tiffany's very proud pronunciation of Mordecai! A "nail in a sure place!"

Then there's my grandson, Wesley. I was in the bedroom with Tiffany having one of our "girl talks" when Wesley knocks on the door. He comes in and I ask him what he's doing. He tells me, "Oh, just walkin' in the hall talkin' to the Holy Ghost."

Another time I asked him if he wanted to pray and he

said, "No thanks. You pray, I'll agree." This was when he was four years old! Every family should be blessed with a Wesley!

Are you getting the picture of what being a "nail in a sure place" means? I sure hope I'm a "nail in a sure place" to my family. I Corinthians 13 tells us of all the gifts we could possibly have, *love* is the greatest. That's a "nail in a sure place!"

Being a "nail in a sure place" speaks of maturity. It denotes a growth pattern which, many times, we do not willingly want to go into. But, there is no shortcut to being what God wants us to be. There is no easy way out of the time of preparation—the time of becoming what we are destined to be in Him. This is the time I've labeled **God's Lamaze**.

Chapter 12

God's Lamaze

And she being with child cried, travailing in birth, and pained to be delivered (Revelation 12:2).

We know this Scripture is not talking about a literal baby being born. This is a spiritual birthing process that is being referred to. We all must go through a birthing process if we are going to give birth to spiritual babies.

We also know that to give birth, there is a certain amount of pain which has to be endured. To help us with this, the Lord gives us what I call *expectant faith.*

When the Lord first spoke to me about teaching on expectant faith and the suddenlys of God, calling it **God's Lamaze**, I thought, "This is going to put me over the brink in my ministry in being labeled a *nut*!" As in the natural, when we go through the Lamaze plan, the birthing process is helped immensely. So it is in the spiritual realm. The Lord told me God's Lamaze will help make the birthing a natural, spiritual experience.

In order for this to happen, we must walk into that

realm of expectant faith. First of all, I want to define what a realm of expectant faith is. This is a place where you *know* something is going to take place even though you don't see it, have any natural indication of its possibility or any evidence that it has ever happened before. *That's a realm of expectant faith!*

Can anyone go to this place? Are we just supposed to *visit* this realm, or does the Lord expect us to *live there*? What examples do we have to encourage us to strive for this realm and what are the directions for getting there?

Now, anyone who knows me very well is aware of the fact that I don't do real well with directions, so for me to ever arrive anywhere, the Lord would have to make it simple and to the point. That's exactly what He's done with the realm of expectant faith.

I remember one time my husband Bob and I were visiting a church to hear an evangelist who was so anointed. He moved prophetically, so I anticipated hearing a word from the Lord. He called me out and began to prophesy to me. He said, "The Lord is going to send you to the North, to the South, to the East and to the West. . . " He proceeded to give me an awesome word from the Lord. I was really blessed by it and on the way home asked Bob what he thought of the prophesy. He said, "Well, the Lord knows if He told you to just go in one direction, you would probably never get there, so He's going to send you in *all* directions to make sure you arrive!" Funny Bob!

We all know the Scripture describing what we think faith is:

Now faith is the substance of things hoped for, the evidence of things not seen. (Hebrews 11:1).

For so many years, I thought the word *now* was a conjunction or a connector word until the day the Holy Spirit spoke to me and said that the "now" in this Scripture is not a conjunction, but an adjective. To be perfectly honest, I didn't remember from my high school days what a conjunction or an adjective was, so I had to look it up. A conjunction is a word that connects sentences. An adjective is a describer. The Lord wanted me to know that He intended for the NOW in this Scripture to relay to His children the kind of faith we need to have in order to walk in that realm of expectancy which will bring results. Let's read the same Scripture in an amplified translation:

Now faith *is the assurance or the title deed of the things hoped for and it's also the conviction that things not yet seen are already possessed by you.* (Amplified).

In Romans 12:3 the Lord tells us He has given to every man *the* measure of faith—*the* indicating a specific amount. In other words, we all start out with the same amount of faith. How, then, can it become *expectant faith*?

Our expectant faith can be likened to pregnancy. Sometimes it is more difficult for a male to receive spiritual things than it is for a woman, simply because a woman was created by God to receive seed. In order for a man to become impregnated with the things of God, he must open himself up to the Spirit of God and overrule the natural and accept the spiritual, becoming a *receiver of seed*. This is necessary for a man to be born again and become a part of the Bride of Christ. He must receive the seed of salvation.

Jesus likened faith to a mustard seed in Matthew 17:20. He said if you have faith the size of a grain of mustard seed, you can speak to a mountain and it be thrown in the sea. Now, that's a pretty powerful statement. The secret to this is a mustard seed, though the least of all the seeds of the earth, when planted, becomes the greatest of all herbs, and the birds of the air use it for a dwelling place (Mark 4:31-32).

The Key: Plant the Seed!

God has planted the seed of the measure of faith in all of us. We have to plant it, or it will never become a tree of *now faith*. You can take a grain of wheat and put it on the shelf, and it will always be just a grain of wheat. You can, however, plant that same grain of wheat and it will become bread for the multitude.

Back when Bob and I had our children, very few men were involved in anything other than the *seed planting*.

Today it isn't like that. You hear, "*We're* going to have a baby" or "*We* start our Lamaze classes next week." I remember when our first granddaughter, Tara Lynn, was born and our son John was telling us how exhausted he was. I asked him if he had gotten a good night's sleep, and he said he hadn't because it had been his turn to get up with the baby. I looked at Bob and said, "Why didn't you tell me *we* were supposed to take turns!" Well, times have changed, folks!

Let's look at some expectant examples in the Word of God. We can't even consider expectant faith without looking at Abraham and Sarah. (This story is found in Genesis 17:15-19 and 18:9-15.) It would seem as though Abraham and Sarah were absolutely faithless by these Scriptures; yet, we know they had at least a small measure of faith. The seed was planted. In verse 12, Sarah scoffs at the idea of their having children; in verse 13, the Lord reveals her scoffing and the *revelation of truth* becomes the water sack that will protect that seed and enable it to grow. When Sarah heard the Lord repeating what she had said (she was so fearful, she lied about laughing), faith leaped in her heart to *believe the unbelievable*. We all know the outcome of the story. Abraham begat Isaac; Isaac begat Jacob; Jacob's name was changed to Israel and the family *became* the nation of God.

Through faith also Sara herself received strength

*to conceive seed, and was delivered of a child
when she was past age, because she judged Him
faithful who had promised* (Hebrews 11:11).

She expected the unexpected!

Faithful is He that calleth you, who also will do it
(I Thessalonians 5:24).

God is faithful! And Sarah believed God. Through
that belief the seed grew, and she gave birth to the
promised manchild. In the same way, we can come to expect the unexpected in today's modern society. Now let's
look at the spiritual side of this.

*. . . But that which is natural; and afterward that
which is spiritual* (I Corinthians 15:46b).

First the natural, then the spiritual. I want you to read
Acts 9:1-16 to get the basis of this story. We need to
know that between verses six and eleven, Paul (who at
this point was still Saul) received instructions which are
not recorded word for word in the book. (He was told
where to go and what to do.)

Saul was knocked off his high horse, blinded by a
"suddenly of God" (which we will look at later) and impregnated with the spiritual baby of taking Jesus to the
Gentiles, before kings and to Israel!

Saul didn't realize he was pregnant with this call. All

he knew was he heard a voice; a blinding light knocked him to the ground; and when he got up, he couldn't see a thing. In the natural, when you first become pregnant, you do not realize the seed has been planted. Usually, the first thing that happens is you get morning sickness. I personally didn't suffer from this, but I understand that most women do. I did find that food affected me differently than in the past. Things I had really enjoyed before had somehow lost their savor. I found it interesting when the Lord pointed out to me that for three days Saul didn't eat or drink anything (v. 9). I called this his "spiritual morning sickness." Saul was so transformed by this encounter with the Lord that his name was changed to Paul. As soon as he realized what had happened, Paul began to tell everyone about Jesus . . . the growing process had begun.

Do you remember how you just couldn't wait to tell everyone you and your mate were going to have a baby? Paul didn't give birth to the promises of God immediately, but spent three years on the back side of the desert (Galatians 1:17-18) allowing the seed that was planted to mature to full stature. When you get pregnant, there are three things which can happen.

1. You Can Abort

Paul says of Demas in II Timothy 4:10a, "For Demas hath forsaken me, having loved this present world. . . " Demas was impregnated with the seed of God, but aborted before it came to full term. I have seen this happen so many times. People get pregnant with a seed of *ministry*, or a seed of *promise*, or a seed of *desire* for something from God, but as soon as the "morning sickness" hits, or the baby begins to form (spiritually speaking), they decide they don't want to be pregnant anymore and get rid of the baby—*spiritual abortion.*

2. Premature Birth

Sometimes if a woman doesn't eat the right food, take the right vitamins, get the proper amount of rest or simply does more than she is able to do in her present condition, she will give birth prematurely. (Of course, there are other reasons for premature birth.)

> *For if a man know not how to rule his own house, how shall he take care of the church of God? Not a novice, lest being lifted up with pride he fall into the condemnation of the devil* (I Timothy 3:5-6).

Now, we know this is making reference in the natural to a man's household, but in the spiritual sense, if a man doesn't rule *this house*—his own temple—and tries to put himself into a place of ministry or authority too soon, the result will be a *premature birth*. We all know preemies have to be incubated, pampered, and eye dropper fed, or they will die.

3. Full Term

As the pregnancy proceeds, the body gets all out of its natural shape. You begin to walk funny, sit funny and you certainly get up and down funny! You begin to get nagging little pains every once in a while, and there just doesn't seem to be any place or position that is comfortable for you to be in. You may even change your mind and say, "I don't want to do this!"

Then the labor begins. When the Lord first told me to call this spiritual exercise *God's Lamaze*, I thought I must surely be losing it this time. In the first place, I knew absolutely nothing about Lamaze except what little bit Ginger (my daughter) had told me. I must admit, I didn't put a whole lot of stock in what she had to say considering their experience. With their first child, Tiffany, Ginger went into labor the week before their Lamaze classes were to start, so they got a crash course in the labor room. With Wesley, they did get through all the classes except the last one which was for C-Section delivery. Guess what? *Wesley was a C-section delivery.* Well, in spite of all this, the Lord spoke to my spirit while I was in prayer about this one day and told me in order to have a healthy baby, we must know how to flow with the pain of delivery and have our focus on Him. When I shared this with Ginger, she said, "Yep, that's Lamaze. Breathe right and have a focus point!" So, I guess there is such a thing as **God's Lamaze**, and He wants us to have a healthy baby.

The problem is, so many don't realize they are pregnant with a spiritual baby. They are just fighting the body changes and the pain and discomfort, and all the while the Lord is saying, "Flow with me, and the birthing will be a natural, spiritual experience." Begin to walk in that realm of expectant faith where you know that you know that you know,

> . . . *that He which hath begun a good work in you will perform it until the day of Jesus Christ* (Philippians 1:6).

> Paul said in Galatians 4:19:
> *My little children, of whom I travail in birth again until Christ be formed in you. . . .*

Paul took it upon himself to *give spiritual birth to the church in Galatia*; to go through the birth pangs for them until Christ was formed in them. How did he do that? What was the spiritual birthing process for this to take place? You can find the answer to this in Romans 8:1-27. You need to read all of this, but we are going to look at a few points to help bring this truth out of the Word. Verse 14 says, "We are the sons of God. . . ." He gave birth to us through the blood and water that came forth from the side of His only begotten Son, Jesus Christ.

You remember back in the very beginning when God looked upon man and saw that he needed a companion? He put man into a deep sleep, opened up his side and brought forth his bride.

Now, I want you to think about what happens when a baby is birthed in the natural. *Blood and water come forth*. What happened when Jesus hung on the cross? His side was opened up with the sword of a soldier, blood and water came forth, and the spiritual bride was born!

Look at verse 18:

> *. . . the sufferings of this present time are not worthy to be compared with the glory. . . .*

After you have a baby, you hold him in your arms for the first time, and he snuggles down into your heart and the sufferings of the moment flee away in light of the baby himself.

What verse 22 is basically saying is, the whole creation is groaning and travailing. *For what?* Verse 23 tells us: ". . . the redemption of our body. . . ." How are we redeemed? *Through Christ.* The world is in travail because of sin. We are in travail because the Holy Spirit within us is making intercession with groanings which cannot be uttered. That is what Paul was talking about in Galatians 4:19 when he said he was travailing in birth until Christ was formed in them! Giving birth is not an easy process. You can get to the very door of the delivery room and have your head say to your body, "I don't want to do this anymore."

The Lord spoke to Jeremiah and gave him quite a picture of the promise of restoration to His people. He used a very graphic illustration, in one instance, to get His point across.

Look at Jeremiah 30:4-6:

And these are the words that the Lord spake concerning Israel and concerning Judah. For thus saith the Lord; We have heard a voice of trembling, of fear, and not of peace. Ask ye now, and see whether a man doth travail with child? Wherefore do I see every man with his hands on his loins, as a woman in travail, and all faces are turned into paleness?

The Lord spoke to Joel and said,

Let the priests, the ministers of the Lord, weep between the porch and the altar, and let them say, Spare thy people, O Lord, and give not thine heritage to reproach, that the heathen should rule over them: wherefore should they say among the people, Where is their God? (Joel 2:17)

He is saying, *travail to give birth*, weep between the porch and the altar. Cry out for My people, oh men of God! To His prophet Hosea, He said,

Afterward shall the children of Israel return, and seek the Lord their God, and David their King; and shall fear the Lord and His goodness in the latter days (Hosea 3:5).

This verse is talking about the redemption of the

Body through the blood of Jesus Christ, who is the Son of David, who sits on the throne, whose scepter shall never depart or be taken away (Genesis 49:10). Hallelujah!

In II Peter chapter 1, we see the promises that are ours as sons of God. He tells us the Lord has given us everything we need that pertains to life (here) and godliness (v. 3). He then tells us to "add to our faith, virtue; and to virtue, knowledge; and to knowledge, temperance; and to temperance, patience; and to patience, godliness; and to godliness, brotherly kindness; and to brotherly kindness, charity"—*God's love (*II Peter 1:5-7).

He goes on to say in verse 8:

For if these things be in you, and abound, they make you that ye shall neither be barren nor unfruitful in the knowledge of our Lord Jesus Christ.

In other words, you have been impregnated with the seed of God, His Word. You are now a son, and you, in return, are expected to bring forth fruit. You are to be neither barren nor unfruitful. *You are commanded by God to give birth!*

Jesus tells us in John 15:16:

Ye have not chosen Me, but I have chosen you and ordained you, that ye should go and bring forth fruit, and that your fruit should remain; that whatsoever ye shall ask of the Father in My Name, He may give it you.

You're pregnant! Are you going to *abort*, give birth *prematurely*, or are you going to learn to walk in the Spirit, hear the voice of the Father, go through the training process (**God's Lamaze**), and bring forth healthy babies? Learn how to flow with the pain and have our focus on Him. Then the birthing process will be a *natural, spiritual experience*.

I am crucified with Christ . . . (Galatians 2:20).

On the way home from a service in another state, I was complaining to Bob and Mikki in the car that I felt like I was birthing something in the realm of the Spirit, and the travailing was more than I really thought I wanted to do. I didn't anymore than get that statement out of my mouth than we passed a billboard which said, "If you want to have a healthy baby, start pushing now." Well, we just about fell apart laughing at God's sense of humor. We never did figure out what the advertisement was for, so I just decided that God knew I was in need of an answer.

You go through the growth, the discomfort, the pain, then **suddenly**. . . .

Chapter 13

The Suddenlys of God

And the Lord, whom ye seek, shall suddenly come to His temple (Malachi 3:1).

We know that we have been impregnated with the seed of God and we are now His sons and the earth is travailing for a manifestation of the redemptive power of His Son, Jesus Christ. We are thereby expected to give birth to fruit that will remain. In order to do that, we must know how to flow with the pain and have our focus on Him. That's walking in the realm of expectant faith and graduating from God's Lamaze Class.

As this process takes place, you will find yourself in a place of spiritual maturity that will produce a more humble spirit in you. The more revelation you get from God, the more you will be required to become the servant of all. Paul started out in II Corinthians 11:5 claiming to be the greatest of the apostles and ended up his ministry in I Timothy 1:15 with the proclamation that he was the chief of sinners. We *must realize* God will give us grace to walk in the authority He has delegated to us. If we try to walk in someone else's delegated authority, we will be at the very least defeated and maybe even destroyed.

Experiencing the "Suddenlys" of God

We need to realize, first of all, that in the beginning, God said—and there was a "suddenly" of God. The earth and all therein *suddenly* appeared. We find the Lord spoke to Noah to go into the ark. He was in there seven days when, *suddenly,* the rains came. Abraham was told to take his promised son up to the mountain of God to offer him as a sacrifice unto the Lord. He is obedient to the voice of God then, *suddenly*, there's a ram caught in the thicket that he was to use as the sacrifice.

We see Moses as he's instructed by God to go before Pharaoh and demand His people be set free from their Egyptian bondage. After all the plagues and deaths, they are finally set free. They get to the Red Sea and find Pharaoh's army hot on their trail. Then, *suddenly,* the Red Sea parts, and they cross on dry ground. Just as *suddenly*, the sea returns to its place to destroy the enemy of the children of God. Joshua marched around the walls of Jericho for seven days, then, *suddenly,* the walls came tumbling down.

Have you noticed how God's "suddenlys" and "forever" can almost be synonymous at times?

> *My thoughts are not your thoughts, neither are your ways My ways, saith the Lord?* (Isaiah 55:8).

It's kinda like having a baby? All you hear is *"Push! Push!"* Then, *suddenly.* . . "Waaaaaaaaa!!!" With every mighty manifestation of God's Spirit comes a *suddenly* of God. For almost 4,000 years, God's people heard about a promised Messiah—a King that would deliver, heal and set the captives free. With great anticipation, certain ones throughout time watched and waited for the prophecies of old to come to pass. Then, *suddenly.* . .

> *And* suddenly *there was with the angel a multitude of the heavenly host praising God; and saying, Glory to God in the highest, and on earth peace, good will toward men?* (Luke 2:13-14, emphasis added)

Jesus came, ministered for approximately three years, was hung on a cross and gave His life. But, *suddenly,* there was a great earthquake, an angel rolled the stone away and the proclamation rang out: *He is risen!* Hallelujah!!

The next "suddenly" I want us to look at is Acts 2:2.

> *And* suddenly *there came a sound from heaven as of a rushing mighty wind, and it filled all the house where they were sitting* (emphasis added).

The disciples had been in the upper room for ten days, when *suddenly.* . .

From Genesis to Revelation, the "suddenlys" of God fill the Bible's pages. Let's look at the suddenlys that are in the future. We've been talking about travailing and the birthing process, so I want to look at I Thessalonians 5:3.

For when they say, Peace and safety; then sudden destruction *cometh upon them, as travail upon a woman with child; and they shall not escape* (emphasis added).

That's one side of God's "suddenlys." There's another side as well.

Behold, I will send My messenger, and he shall prepare the way before Me: and the Lord, whom ye seek, shall suddenly *come to His temple* (Malachi 3:1, emphasis added).

What? Know ye not that you are the Temple of the Lord? He goes on to say that He is going to purify the sons of Levi—the priesthood, the ministry—*then* the offering of Judah, the *praise of His people*, will be pleasant and acceptable unto the Lord.

It came even to pass, as the trumpeters and singers were as one, to make one sound to be heard in praising and thanking the Lord, and when they lifted up their voice with the trumpets and cymbals and instruments of music, and praised the Lord, *saying, For He is good; for His mercy endureth for ever: that then [**suddenly**] the house was filled with a cloud, even the house of the Lord; So that the priests could not stand to minister by reason of the cloud: for the glory of the Lord had filled the house of God?* (II Chronicles 5:13-14, emphasis added)

The priests couldn't stand. That is what we refer to as being *slain in the Spirit.*

Know ye not that ye are the temple of God, and that the Spirit of God dwelleth in you? (I Corinthians 3:16)

Paul is asking a question here. Don't you *know* this? He then makes a statement:

If any man defile the temple of God, him shall God destroy? for the temple of God is Holy, which temple ye are? (I Corinthians 3:17)

God is preparing a remnant who are going to walk in that special place of *expectancy* and who are going to produce the last day manifestation of God's glory which *He* called the combined rains of the former and latter day rains. He is going to *suddenly* come into His Temple and His glory will *suddenly* fill the place.

Anyone who has ever heard me teach or minister has

heard me talk about the importance of being ready. You have heard me say, "When the day comes, if you are not in, then you will be left out! For years I have been giving warning that what is about to happen will happen quickly. The remnant for the manifested "suddenlys" of God are even now being prepared!

Even so then at this present time also there is a remnant according to the election of grace (Romans 11:5).

The Revelation of Jesus Christ, which God gave to him [John] *to show unto His servants things which must shortly come to pass . . .* (Revelation 1:1).

That word "shortly" means, once it begins, it will happen *suddenly.*

And the dragon was wroth with the woman [church], *and went to make war with the remnant of her seed, which keep the commandments of God, and have the testimony of Jesus Christ* (Revelation 12:17).

That's us!

I know I'm giving you a lot of Scripture right now, but we need to understand who we are in Him. The Son of God became the Son of Man so that sons of men could become sons of God!

Is there a *realm of expectant faith* that will give birth to the "suddenlys" of God? Yes—*if* you are willing to pay the price. That means having a clean, holy temple for the Lord to take up His abode in and walking in obedience to His Word. You notice in every instance that God's promises became a *suddenly* of God, obedience came first.

Can we expect the unexpected in today's modern society? Yes—*if* you are willing to pay the price by having a clean, holy temple for the Lord to take up His abode in and walk in obedience to His Word.

Can this power and anointing be released in you? Yes—if you are willing to pay the price by having a clean, holy temple for the Lord to take up His abode in and walk in obedience to His Word. *Are you getting the message?* As you do this, you *become* that remnant, who, like the disciples of old, came down out of the upper room after the wind of the Holy Ghost *suddenly* filled their temple, to walk in that realm of expectant faith *so powerful* that the shadow of Peter had so much of the glory of God radiating from it that *the people he passed on the street were instantly healed.* Peter could then go up to the lame man at the gate Beautiful and say:

Silver and gold have I none; but such as I have give I thee: In the name of Jesus Christ of Nazareth rise up and walk (Acts 3:6).

We, the last day remnant of God's army whom He is

raising up, are right now in birth pangs. We're getting delivered from works of the flesh; we're birthing seeds of God's revelatory truths; *we're in the process of birthing the presence of God filling the temple.* S*uddenly* we're going to walk in the power, anointing and glory of the Almighty as His Sons, His Bride, His overcoming army, victorious in Him!

The Lord told Daniel that the people who *know their God* shall be strong and *do exploits* (Daniel 11:32).

". . . Know their God"—that's having expectant faith!

". . . Shall be strong and do exploits. . ."—that's expectant faith which produces the "suddenlys" of God!

Chapter 14

His Manifested Glory

Christ in you, the hope of glory (Colossians 1:27).

We get excited thinking about the manifested glory of the Lord being wrought upon us. We have this glamorous idea of what that means, but most of us don't even bother to check it out with the Word of God. We are going to see two sides of God's glory in this chapter.

We already know there is a realm of expectant faith which will produce in us the "suddenlys" of God if we are willing to pay the price. What I want us to realize now is, the "suddenlys" of God will produce the manifested glory.

Repent ye therefore, and be converted, that your sins may be blotted out, when the times of refreshing shall come from the presence of the Lord; And He shall send Jesus Christ, which before was preached unto you: Whom the heaven must receive until the times of restitution of all things, which

God hath spoken by the mouth of all His holy prophets since the world began (Acts 3:19-21).

The Amplified Bible says in verse 21, ". . . whom heaven must receive (and retain). . . " In other words, He can't come back until this is done.

We understand that from the beginning, with the fall of man, open communion with God was lost. Because of that fall, sin entered into the heart of man; and the man became the ruler over the woman. Because of that sin, the woman conceived and gave birth to two sons, Cain and Abel. We find in Genesis 4:1-2 that Eve conceived once but bore twice.

Godly character was found in Abel; and sin, jealousy, anger and murder in the other son, Cain. From that time on, sin became ruler over man. God found a righteous man later in Noah; but again, sin entered into the hearts of men. All through the Word, we see God longing for and seeking a people who would enter into His rest; who would *long* for a time of refreshing in Him. But, by and large, they were few and far between. . . a David here, a Deborah there. . . We know the eventual answer was God becoming man and giving Himself for our atonement. All He ever really wanted was a people who would bring glory and honor to His Name. In Isaiah 43:7, He tells us we were created for His glory. *Why are we here?* **To bring glory to the Father!** So, what's the answer? How can we bring glory to the Father? How can we walk in His Manifested Glory?

One of the meanings of the word "glory" in the Hebrew is: "to make heavy; burdensome, weight; be grievous." That makes us take a different view of the word "glory," doesn't it? Paul said:

For I reckon that the sufferings of this present time are not worthy to be compared with the glory which shall be revealed in us (Romans 8:18).

The Lord also says in Proverbs 25:2, ". . . It is the glory of God to conceal a thing. . . "

We have something that is to *be revealed* and we have something that is concealed. So, *where does God hide His glory?*

We need to understand, God does not purposely hide things from us in order to tantalize us and make us feel that we can't comprehend. It is for a generous purpose, and meant to assure us that as quickly (or slowly sometimes) and as surely as we can bear it, the full revelation of God will be made clear. Can't you just hear Him saying to the children of Israel, "one more time around the mountain!"?

The secret things belong unto the Lord our God; but those things which are revealed belong unto us and to our children for ever, that we may do all the words of this law (Deuteronomy 29:29).

So how does God *reveal His glory?*

1. Obedience

God reveals His glory in the teaching of obedience. It is only by obedience we understand the teachings of God. Have I always obeyed God in the little things? Fasting, letting go of a habit He is speaking to me about or just being faithful to attend church? Have I gotten grounded in Him and am I doing the work God has called me to do, or have I gotten my feelings hurt, been offended and just changed churches because that was the easier way out?

One of the fruits of the Spirit is *longsuffering*. This word means "not getting your feelings easily hurt." If this is the case in your life, you will never fathom the mysteries of God. By obeying the truth that has been *revealed to you*, you will have a little more of God's glory revealed in your life.

2. Experience

Experience is a gateway of understanding, not an end in itself.

> *Therefore being justified by faith, we have peace with God through our Lord Jesus Christ: By whom also we have access by faith into this grace wherein we stand, and rejoice in hope of the glory of God. And not only so, but we glory in tribulations also: knowing that tribulation worketh patience; And patience experience; and experience hope; And hope maketh not ashamed; because the*

love of God is shed abroad in our hearts by the Holy Ghost which is given unto us (Romans 5:1-5).

Now, I realize that I'm giving you a lot of Scripture, but this is too important to miss!

We can be bound by the very experience that was meant to lead us into the secrets of God. The faith of many spiritual Christians is eclipsed today because they have boxed themselves in by the experience, instead of allowing the experience—illness, emotional battles, finances, family problems *whatever the case may be*—move them into the light of God. God wants us to get to the place where *He holds completely and absolutely*, and experience doesn't hinder us, but only becomes a stepping stone to His glory being revealed.

The reality of Colossians 1:27b, "Christ in you, the hope of glory. . ." Total relief—the burden is gone—no conscious experience left, because Jesus Christ is all in all. Can this be done and if so, *how*?

Come unto Me, all ye that labor and are heavy laden, and I will give you rest. Take My yoke upon you, and learn of Me; for I am meek and lowly in heart: and ye shall find rest unto your souls. For My yoke is easy, and My burden is light (Matthew 11:28-30).

3. Trials

God has hidden the glory of His teachings in the experience of temptations, or various trials.

*My brethren, count it all joy when ye fall into
divers temptations; Knowing this, that the trying
of your faith worketh patience. But let patience
have her perfect work, that ye may be perfect and
entire, wanting nothing. If any of you lack
wisdom, let him ask of God, that giveth to all men
liberally, and upbraideth not; and it shall be given
him* (James 1:2-5).

The Lord is telling us that He doesn't resent our asking
Him for His wisdom. *That's God's hidden manna!*

*Blessed is the man that endureth temptation: for
when he is tried, he shall receive the crown of life,
which the Lord hath promised to them that love
Him* (James 1:12).

God wants us to learn to thank Him for our *tried faith*, because it works *patience*. Tried faith is spendable. It is
wealth laid up in heaven; it will reveal God's glory in us
if we let it.

4. Times Of Darkness

God reveals His glory in times of darkness. Hebrews
12:11 tells us that ". . . no chastening for the present
seemeth to be joyous." But, we are also told by the
prophet Isaiah that God will give us treasures of darkness
(Isaiah 45:3).

There is nothing more wearying to the eyes than

perpetual sunshine. The same is true spiritually. The valley of the shadow gives us time to reflect, and we learn to praise God because it is in the valley that He restores our soul. It takes two valleys to make one mountain. There has to be one on each side of the mountain, or it won't be a mountain. All perpetual sunshine creates deserts. What are the times in our lives that have furthered us the most? The days of green pastures or the valleys?

It is in the valley where the comforting, restoring and sustaining hand of God reveals *His* glory. When I am weak, then I am strong.

> *For our light affliction, which is but for a moment, worketh for us a far more exceeding and eternal weight of glory; While we look not at the things which are seen, but at the things which are not seen: for the things which are seen are temporal; but the things which are not seen are eternal* (II Corinthians 4:17-18).

We have the glory of God being revealed in *obedience*, *experience*, *trials* and *times of darkness*. Are you still as excited about having His glory revealed in you?

There is a description of the promises of God for His children in Isaiah 35 that will stir our soul to say, "Here am I Lord, send me." Remember, the Old Testament is a type and shadow of the New Covenant (Isaiah 35:1-10).

In the wilderness of Israel, there are snakes, scorpions,

death and drought. The Lord is saying this is symbolic of the believer who is living in a place of spiritual drought with the powers of darkness being an ever-present problem (snakes, scorpions, etc.). But, the glory of Lebanon, the excellency of Carmel and Sharon, is going to burst forth. That's the fragrance of the Holy Spirit (cedars of Lebanon), the fertile ground of Carmel and Sharon, the most fertile ground in the Middle East, a fresh revelation of God's Word that will bear much fruit. Verse 2 says, ". . . They shall see the glory of the Lord. . ." a new vision of God's glory! Verses 3-6 tell of a great revival of miracles and healings which will take place. Verse 7 says: ". . . the parched ground shall become a pool, and the thirsty land springs of water. . . . " That's the anointing of the Holy Spirit which will burst forth with rivers of living water to a dry and thirsty land. There is going to be a highway of holiness God's people will walk on which will produce divine protection from the dragons (demonic forces)!

Finally, we see in verse 10 the ransomed of the Lord returning to Zion with joy and gladness, and sorrow shall flee away. Glory!

I believe the beginning of this return began on the day of Pentecost and has been "being worked" ever since to bring us to the appointed time of Jesus' return to earth. The Holy Spirit has done a work in them who were willing, and *all things* to the Bride of Christ has been restored! Hallelujah!

At this time, we will surely have entered into His

times of refreshing in spite of trials, circumstances or tribulations. We are told in Hebrews 4 to ". . . labor therefore to enter into that rest."

The other side of the manifested glory, *to them who have paid the price*, include *miracles, power, joy, peace, anointing* like we've never seen. Has this happened sporadically with anointed men and women of God? And if so, how can we learn from their mistakes?

Chapter 15

Touching the Bones of Faith

And Elisha died, and they buried him. And the bands of the Moabites invaded the land at the coming in of the year. And it came to pass, as they were burying a man, that, behold, they spied a band of men; and they cast the man into the sepulchre of Elisha: and when the man was let down, and touched the bones of Elisha, he revived, and stood up on his feet (II Kings 13:20-21).

What a story! Elisha's bones had so much life in them, this unnamed man sprang to his feet, filled with new life! This fulfilled the "double portion" word of Elijah to Elisha, that, even in death, he raised more from the dead than Elijah had done.

A writer by the name of Steve Thompson said it this way:

In the same way, as we uncover and "touch the bones of faith" of the great heroes of faith who have preceded us, we can also be spiritually revived.

106

One of the definitions of "bone" is "the essence or core of something." The bones also contain marrow, which produces the life-giving blood. Prophetically then, *touching the bones* speaks of discovering the essence of what produced the life and vigor of those who have preceded us in faith.

We don't think anything about going to the great faith chapter in Hebrews 11 and recounting the faith and lives of the great men and women of God through the Word. Yet, we sometimes miss the history of faith-building giants whom God has since provided for us—to "touch their bones," to receive new life that will cause us to burst forth from our lifeless state. We sometimes allow what we consider traditions of men, religious doctrines and denominational walls to keep us from the great, revealed truths of God that were used to change the hearts of men through people like John Wesley, Martin Luther, Smith Wigglesworth, Amy Simple McPhearson and Kathryn Kulman.

There are many bones in church history we need to touch, and a man by the name of Alfred Goodrich Garr is one of them. He was reportedly the first white man to receive the baptism in the Holy Ghost during the Azuza Street Revival at the turn of the century.

He was born in 1874 into a family which had been very wealthy, but lost everything in the financial panic of 1860 that brought many to a level of overnight poverty. His father died when he was eight years old. So that left him and his mother alone, as the other children were grown and on their own. At this time, a revival began in the Baptist church in his town, and he was the first one to go forward to accept Jesus. Although he was baptized and joined the church, when another revival would come to town, he continued to be the first to go forward. His pastor tried to convince him that he was already saved, but he insisted he was "feeling for God," as he put it. This went on for years until at the age of 15, Alfred went into the woods to pray and "feel for God." The Lord revealed Himself to Alfred in a way that would forever change his life. He was filled with a peace that passed all under-standing and when he came home, his mother knew something had happened. She knew Alfred had found a place in God he had not had before. From age eight to age fifteen, Alfred Garr had an insatiable hunger for the Lord that *consumed* him. This is the first of the "bones of faith" we need to touch—*his hunger for God!*

After this experience, Alfred was fervent in his desire to bring others to the Lord. It is said of him that what he did couldn't be considered preaching. He simply spoke a little, cried a little and prayed a little, and the Lord used him to change entire communities. In the midst of all of this, he still had hunger for more of God, which led him to enroll in Bible College.

He married Lillian, the daughter of a Methodist Bishop, and they later moved to California where they began to pastor a small church called the Burning Bush Congregation. The Lord was surely directing every step they took. He eventually met a one-eyed black man by the name of William Seymore who was holding services in a run-down mission on Azuza Street. William Seymore had touched the bones of faith of a man named Charles Parham, who had a Bible School in Topeka, Kansas. He wasn't allowed to go into the classroom himself because he was black, so he would sit outside and listen to Brother Parham teach about the power of the Holy Ghost which was unheard of to most people.

In Seymore's own words he said:

Before I met Parham, such a hunger was in my heart that I prayed for five hours a day for two and a half years. I got to Los Angeles and that hunger was not less, but more. I prayed, "God, what can I do?" The Spirit said, "Pray more. There are better things to be had in the spiritual life, but they must be sought out with faith and prayer." "But Lord, I'm praying five hours a day now." I increased my hours of prayer to seven and prayed on for a year and a half more. I prayed to God to give me what Parham had preached, the *real* Holy Ghost and fire with tongues and love and power of God like the apostles had (*Morning Star Journal,* Vol.4, #4).

Seymore, like Garr, was empowered primarily through the agency of his deep spiritual hunger for God.

Garr began visiting Azuza Street Mission, and although there was gossip, ridicule and persecution going on by the established churches that prevented any "respectable Christian" from going there, Garr's hunger for more of the Lord pushed him on. His church turned him out, and his wife was going to leave him, but he simply trusted God to do whatever needed to be done. He convinced his wife to visit the mission just once before leaving him, and as they were walking down the aisle, the power of God hit her and she began praising God. She was baptized in the Holy Ghost and although Alfred, himself, had not received, he rejoiced with her and continued to trust the Lord.

Here is another *bone* of his life we need to touch. The grace to *trust God* with His people instead of us trying to manipulate them into a relationship.

Later, when many of the Pentecostal denominations began to get legalistic in their beliefs, Garr never compromised his belief that God changes man from the *inside out* instead of the outside in. The Lord lets us know in Matthew 15:19 that it is not the things which are on the outside that defiles, it's what comes from the inside.

When I was in Mexico with some friends several years ago, we had an interesting incident happen on a tour bus going to see the Mayan ruins of Chichen Itza. On the way back, the tour guide was having people on the bus get up and sing a song. Everyone was laughing and having fun with this, as there were people from all over the world on this tour. We heard people from Poland, Russia, Canada and of course Mexico, singing in their native language. I knew we would end up at the front of that bus before the trip was over, so I was trying to think of a song we could sing if that happened. I had what I consider to be one of the most phenomenal "brain drains" possible during that time. I could not think of one song except "Amazing Grace." Well, the inevitable happened and when the guide called on us, I explained to him that we sang Gospel music. He said that was okay, go ahead and sing our song. I thought to myself, "Boy, this is going to go over like a lead balloon." But, we began to sing "Amazing Grace" to a packed bus, going through the middle of a jungle, to a bunch of people who, for the most part, couldn't even speak English. Before we knew it, several others began to sing with us, although they were singing in a different language. When the bus stopped for a break, a couple from Canada was waiting for us outside the bus. They came up and told us how much they enjoyed our song, and the man began to give me his testimony. I told him I couldn't think of a single song to sing except "Amazing Grace." He said something that spoke to my spirit in such a way that I'll never forget it. He said, "Well, what's inside is what is going to come out. You just have to be what you are."

I remembered the Lord teaching me about *being* a witness. Jesus said that we would receive power to be His witness, after the power of the Holy Ghost came upon us. The Lord then asked me if I had to *decide to be a woman* when I got up in the morning. I thought, "How silly, of course not because I *am* a woman." The Lord then reiterated the fact that *I am His witness.* It isn't something I have to try to do; it's something I am. What I am inside is what had to come out on that bus. I'm just an example of

His amazing grace. It was exciting how something as simple as a song changed the entire atmosphere of that trip. I know lives were touched and changed by the Spirit of God who traveled on that bus.

Brother Garr knew that most who are truly touched by Jesus are *forever ruined* for anything else. He was later baptized with the Holy Ghost and as he was praising God, a British Indian came into the meeting and inquired as to how he had learned to speak his native Bengali language. Although he didn't realize he was speaking Bengali, Brother Garr took that as a direct sign from the Lord that he was to go to India as a missionary. Another *bone* we need to touch from this mighty man of God is his *sense of urgency* to obey. His motto was, "Get Started Now." He simply believed he was to obey God *quickly* —not impulsively—and upon doing so, God would provide the rest of the plan. Most people don't know the difference between quick obedience and impulsive action. With quick obedience, you think about the instructions you have received and act on them quickly, while on the other hand, an impulsive act is action *without thought.*

Dr. Garr's method of ministry was to simply infect people with his hunger for God, and then direct them to the Well of Living Water, Jesus.

As a result of his intense hunger for the Lord, Brother Garr would not be stopped by discouragement. He knew in his heart the powerful truth that "God is a rewarder of them that *diligently seek Him*" (Hebrews 11:6).

With this faith, he and his family left for India in 1907

to take the message of the Holy Ghost to the people there. When they arrived, they found that all their luggage had been stolen; all they had were the carrying cases they held in their hands. He rented a cheap room and found they had enough money for breakfast the next morning. Resting in the knowledge that God had sent them, he also knew God would provide all they needed.

The next morning after breakfast, they were in prayer when a British officer by the name of Captain Angelsmith arrived at their door. I found it interesting that his name was *Angel*-smith. He asked if there was a man by the name of Garr there. He then went on to tell them how, that morning, while in prayer, the Lord had spoken to him giving him Garr's name and the address where they were staying. He told him to take a bag of gold sovereigns to him as a gift. This, of course, poured fuel on the already flaming heart of this young missionary and his family. He went on to take the message of the Holy Ghost to Tibet, Hong Kong, China and Japan. His faith was greatly tested with the death of his two daughters and the near death of his wife and infant son at birth. Because of the intense hatred for foreigners, they were eventually forced to return to America. This too proved to be the hand of God as he was soon preaching to thousands in Los Angeles. Although he had come through many tests, his greatest was yet to come.

At the height of his success, Alfred Garr found he had stomach cancer, became bedridden, and in a very short time, was unable to eat but a few spoonfuls of liquid a day. Instead of becoming hungry for natural food, he became hungry for spiritual food: the healing power of God's Word. Brother Garr was miraculously healed and within a few months was preaching a new-found power: *Jesus is a healing Jesus!*

He was the first to use a tent to carry the Gospel all over the country and Canada. He ministered with Aimee Simple McPherson in her Angeles Temple, and they remained close friends for the remainder of his life. His wife passed away, and he eventually married an old family friend, Hannah. She was used greatly by God in a radio ministry. They built a church in Charlotte, N.C., where they remained until his death. His congregation pioneered the use of television for preaching the Gospel message and began what would later become the PTL Television Network.

Touching the bones of faith of a man named Alfred Goodrich Garr: What did he have that we can glean from as Elisha did from Elijah?

1. He had a hunger for God
He *knew* that ". . . them that hunger for righteousness shall be filled" (Matthew 5:6).

2. He was a great man of prayer
He *knew* that the ". . . Effectual fervent prayer of a righteous man availeth much" (James 5:16b).

3. He trusted God in everything
He *knew* ". . . his God would supply all his needs

according to His riches in glory by Christ Jesus"
(Philippians 4:19).

4. He walked with a sense of urgency to obey
He *knew* that ". . . obedience is better than sacrifice"
(I Samuel 15:22b).

5. He never lost his faith
He *knew* that ". . . without faith it is impossible to
please God" (Hebrews 11:6b).

6. *He lived the Word!*
Does this sound like a modern day Paul or Elijah or
Elisha? Or "your name?" I told the Lord that if I go on to
be with Him before He comes back to earth, I want my
bones to leave behind so much power of Him in them,
that I too will continue to "raise the dead" with the reve-
lations of God that have been passed on to others. I want
to so *infect* people with the things of God that there will
be an epidemic of the Gospel of Jesus Christ! Then I can
say, with the Apostle Paul, "I have fought a good fight, I
have finished my course, I have kept the faith"
(II Timothy 4:7). I want to touch some bones of faith and
change the lives of others and help prepare them for **His
final outpouring**.

Chapter 16

His Final Outpouring

I will pour out of My Spirit upon all flesh (Acts 2:17).

In the final outpouring of God's Spirit, there are going to be three distinct groups of people pertaining to the kingdom of God. There will be, first of all, that group which will simply dismiss it.

In Luke 16:19-31, we have the story of the rich man and the beggar named Lazarus. The rich man is in torment because he did not receive the truths of God when he had the opportunity. He was just concerned with acquiring more things in this life. He simply *dismissed* the things of the Lord. He begs for Father Abraham to *do something* about the situation, but he can't; it's too late. He then asks him to send Lazarus back to tell his brothers not to make the same mistake he made. Look at verses 28-31:

For I have five brethren; that he may testify unto

116

*them, lest they also come into this place of tor-
ment. Abraham saith unto him, They have Moses
and the prophets; let them hear them. And he
said, Nay, father Abraham: but if one went unto
them from the dead, they will repent. And he said
unto him, If they hear not Moses and the
prophets, neither will they be persuaded, though
one rose from the dead.*

Even if one went back from the dead to tell them, *they
would still just dismiss it.*

*If our gospel be hid, it is hid to them that are lost:
In whom the god of this world hath blinded the
minds of them which believe not, lest the light of
the glorious gospel of Christ, who is the image of
God, should shine unto them* (II Corinthians 4:3-4).

You remember the story in I Kings 18, when Elijah
told his servant that he heard the sound of an abundance
of rain? The servant's response: "There is nothing."

It will be the same in this Last Day Outpouring. There
will be those who will hear nothing, see nothing, receive
nothing, and do nothing. *They will just dismiss it.*

The next group we will see are those who will just
discuss it. In Luke 18:18-23, we have the story of the rich
young ruler. He asked the question, "What shall I do to
inherit eternal life?" (v. 18). Jesus then began to tell him
what he needed to do. This young man discussed all that

Jesus told him. When it came down to the final decision, all he did was *discuss it*.

> *Sell all that thou hast and distribute unto the poor.*
> *. . when he heard this, he was very sorrowful: for*
> *he was very rich* (vs. 22-23).

He was a hearer of the Word, but not a doer.

In the second chapter of Acts we have two questions being asked by the people standing around. In Acts 2:12 they are asking, "What meaneth this?" They have seen the power of the Holy Ghost that was upon Peter and the others as they came down out of the upper room, and they want to know, "What does this mean?" In other words, *"What are these crazy Christians doing now?"*

But, there is another group asking another question (v. 37). They are saying "What shall we do?" What must we do to walk with the Lord? Two groups: the group that was willing to *discuss it* and the group that was willing to *declare it*.

In this last-day outpouring, there will be a great multitude who are going to be willing to stand and *declare* the truths of God. In Acts 4, we have a good example to follow. Peter and John are telling the people they need to repent and believe on the Lord Jesus Christ. In verse 13 it says they *marveled* and realized Peter and John had been with Jesus. The *religious* of the day began to plan how to stop them from drawing the people toward becoming followers of Jesus. They commanded Peter and John not to speak at all nor teach in the name of Jesus (v. 18). But Peter had the anointing of declaration on him. He began to pray, and verse 29 says, "And now, Lord, behold their threatenings: and grant unto Thy servants, that with all boldness they may speak Thy Word." He made up his mind that, in spite of their threats, in spite of the danger to their lives, they *would declare the truths of the Lord.*

The Lord is raising up a people who are going to stand strong for Him! They are going to realize He has brought them in to send them out! We have seen a great move in this last decade of the Spirit of God upon the young people. The youth in the Kansas City Fellowship are children prophesying and laying hands on the sick. The teens in the Toronto Blessing are moving out to declare their faith in the resurrected Christ. The young people who are gong on mission trips to places like China, Russia, Africa and other foreign lands are going because the *call of God is upon them to declare His mighty works.*

The Lord spoke to a young man by the name of Jeremiah and said:

> . . . *Say not, I am a child: for thou shalt go to all that I shall send thee, and whatsoever I command thee thou shalt speak* (Jeremiah 1:7).

The Lord then said in verse 12:

> . . . *For I will hasten My Word to perform it.*

Don't worry about a thing, Jerry: I will make it happen.

> *Be glad then, ye children of Zion, and rejoice in the Lord your God: for He hath given you the former rain moderately, and He will cause to come down for you the rain, the former rain, and the latter rain in the first month* (Joel 2:23).

The Lord is saying to us, "In the very first month that the rain begins to fall upon My people, I will send it in the fullness that I have promised."

> *Then shall we know, if we follow on to know the Lord: His going forth is prepared as the morning; and He shall come unto us as the rain, as the latter and the former rain unto the earth* (Hosea 6:3).

This is the key: *We must follow on to know the Lord.* He's brought us in *to send us out* into a world of darkness to declare the works of the Lord. Jesus said to His disciples, "Go ye therefore. . . "

Jesus is coming back for a *glorious* Church! A Church without *spot* or *wrinkle*! A Church that is holy and without any blemish.

Does this sound like a church as we know it now? Do you and I fill the bill? Can we manage to get into the mold which we see the Word of God proclaiming the bride must fit into?

How Is This Ever Going to Happen?

Throughout time, He has had a people. We can see the *Joshua generation* in Joshua 5 and 6. They were a remnant the Lord had brought out of Egyptian bondage, but they were to prove to be a *radical remnant*. When the Lord said, "Be silent," they were silent. When He said, "March," they marched. When He said "Shout!" they shouted. When He said, "I've given you the land," they went in and possessed it. When the voice of the Lord said, "Victory!" *this Joshua generation believed*!

Then we can see Gideon's Army in Judges 7:3-8. He started out with 32,000 men. Can you imagine an army that size under the command of one man who has never done this before? The Lord tells him that 22,000 of them are cowards, and he is to send them back home. He then finds out that, of the 10,000 who were left, 9,700 of them were so self-centered, they were more concerned about their personal comfort and needs and they were not ready to face the enemy. God said, "Get rid of them." This took Gideon from the place of having a mighty army of 32,000 to having a meager handful of 300 men.

If we pastored a church that had 32,000 today and had a split with only 300 remaining, we would surely be accused of having missed God, wouldn't we? But, Gideon's army *knew the voice of the Lord!* They obeyed and the Lord gave them the victory. The enemy turned against themselves and the victory was won because of the 300

men that fought with Gideon. With swords? No! With
obedience!

I would rather have 30 people who would share my
vision from the Lord and stand with me in prayer and
obedience to God, than have 1,000 faithful tithers who
sow discord and strife as they give their almighty dollars.

Give me Gideon's army any day!

Chapter 17

The Final Call

Multitudes, multitudes, in the valley of decision (Joel 3:14).

We have seen the radical remnant who were the "Joshua Generation," and we have looked at Gideon's army, now let's look at another group of people who will help teach us how to become that Bride that wears combat boots.

The Elijah Company

In I Kings 18:7-46 we have the story of a company of people who changed the history of a nation and people because they believed God. We have Obadiah, who greatly feared the Lord and was hiding prophets of God from the hand of King Ahab and the wicked queen, Jezebel. He came upon Elijah (v. 7) and Elijah proceeds to tell him to ". . . go, tell thy lord (Ahab), Behold, Elijah is here!"

Can you imagine the nerve of this man? They have been looking everywhere for him to kill him and be rid of this menace once and for all. He proceeds to go to Ahab and make himself and his intentions known. Ahab says in verse 17, "Are you that trouble maker?" Let me ask you, does the devil recognize you as a trouble maker to his kingdom? King Ahab says, "Are you the one who, for three and a half years, has held back the rain and brought drought upon my kingdom?" Elijah then turns the tables on him and informs him it is *his own sin* and the sin of his fathers for forsaking the God of Israel that has brought the curse upon the land.

In verse 19 Elijah tells King Ahab to get all his mighty prophets together with the people so they can see just who is the mighty God of Israel.

Elijah tells the people in verse 21, "It's time for the *final call.* . . If Baal be god, then serve him. But, if this god cannot do what needs to be done, then *choose the God that can!*"

He allows the 450 prophets of Baal to choose the bullock, cut it up, put it on the altar, *but they can't start the fire.* Their god has to *be* the fire which will consume the sacrifice. The Word of God says they called upon Baal from morning until noon crying out for him to hear them. They got so distraught they jumped up and down on the altar and broke it to pieces. Elijah mocked them and said, "Cry a little louder. Maybe your god is busy talking to someone, or just stepped out for a moment; or maybe he is on vacation or is asleep and needs to be wakened!"

(v. 27). The prophets got so upset, they began to cut themselves and cry out to their god even more. Evening came and what has happened? *Absolutely nothing*, except they have broken down the altar, and Elijah has to repair it before he can offer up his sacrifice to God.

Elijah takes 12 stones, representing the 12 tribes of Israel, puts the wood in order, cuts up the bullock and lays it on the altar, and has a trench dug around the entire sacrifice. He then says, "Fill four barrels with water and pour it on the burnt sacrifice and on the wood." They did this three times until the wood, the sacrifice and the trench were running over with water.

Now, I want to look at what Elijah did in detail. Chapter 18:36-38 says:

And it came to pass at the time of the offering of the evening sacrifice, that Elijah the prophet came near, and said, Lord God of Abraham, Isaac and of Israel, let it be known this day that Thou art God in Israel, and that I am Thy servant, and that I have done all these things at Thy Word. Hear me, O Lord, hear me, that this people may know that Thou art the Lord God, and Thou hast turned their heart back again. Then the fire of the Lord fell, and consumed the burnt sacrifice, and the wood, and the stones, and the dust, and licked up the water that was in the trench.

When the fire fell from heaven, the people fell on

their faces and cried out, "The Lord, He is the God. . . the Lord, He is the God." In this, the final call of the Lord, there is going to be another Elijah company who is going to stand up strong! That Elijah company is going to boldly present itself in the face of the enemy and announce, like Elijah of old, "I am here" and if need be, call down fire from heaven and proclaim, "He is Lord!"

The Lord is sounding the final call for that strong, faith-believing, Joshua generation; for that obedient Gideon's army; for that boldness of the Elijah company! Strong! Obedient! Bold! What will this group of people be?

That He might present it to Himself a glorious church, not having spot, or wrinkle, or any such thing; but that it should be holy and without blemish (Ephesians 5:27).

Oh Lord, let our cry be:

That I may know Him, and the power of His resurrection, and the fellowship of His sufferings, being made conformable unto His death (Philippians 3:10).

Can we do this? The answer is *Yes! Yes! **Yes!*** Jesus made the way for this glorious Church, His Bride, to be fully formed *in Him.*

Being confident of this very thing, that He which

hath begun a good work in you will perform it until the day of Jesus Christ (Philippians 1:6).

The *Living Bible* says it this way:

And I am sure that God who began the good work in you will keep right on helping you to grow in His grace until His task within you is finally finished on that day when Jesus Christ returns (Philippians 1:6).

For it is God which worketh in you both to will and to do of His good pleasure (Philippians 2:13).

He'll give us the "want" to, and then help us to accomplish it! That's God! He's getting the Bride ready: prepared for the wedding; prepared for the war. That's the bride wearing combat boots.

Are you getting the picture? Are you beginning to see that we must be prepared for whatever comes our way? Do you understand that we will have to face the enemy one way or the other? Until the Bride has this understanding, she will never be at the place of being able to say, in unison:

Lord Jesus, Come!

Chapter 18

Let the Bride Say, "Come"

Even so, Come, Lord Jesus (Revelation 22:20b).

We must realize that we are on the brink of spiritual destiny. The Lord has been preparing us (His Bride) for His return for generations. There are four truths we must have to enter into God's end-time strategy:

1. **We must know we are *God's people of destiny*.**
2. **We must realize that we are in *the Final Countdown*.**
3. **We must realize that we are in a *time of crisis*.**
4. **We must know we have *nothing to fear*.**

There *is* persecution coming to the Church. *Why?* The same reason they were against Jesus. The lame are going to walk, the deaf are going to hear, the blind are going to see and the dead are going to be raised.

In Mark 14:37, we find the disciples sleeping at a most crucial moment. This is a message to the Church today. *We must wake up*! What was good enough or allowed for the Church yesterday is not going to be good enough for today. *We are a distinct people, for a specific time for a divine purpose! We must be prepared for the coming war!* We are in the army of God! We truly are on the brink of spiritual destiny.

> *The Revelation of Jesus Christ, which God gave unto Him, to shew unto His servants things which must shortly come to pass; and He sent and signified it by His angel unto His servant John* (Revelation 1:1).

The Lord is saying here that once it begins, it will happen quickly. ". . . those things which must *shortly* come to pass. . ." In Mark 13:30-37, we have a word from the Lord, Himself, giving us instructions. The key verse for this is verse 37: ". . . And what I say unto you I say unto all, *watch.. . . .*"

Message to the Church: Set a Watch

You are in the army of the Lord and there are rules for all military:

1. **Be constantly alert.**
2. **Watch for the enemy.**
3. **Guard the camp.**
4. **Sound the alarm to give warning.**
5. ***Stop* the enemy at all costs.**

The Church has not prepared for the coming of the Lord. Those who fail to hear what the Spirit of the Lord is saying will fall. The time for the return of Jesus was set at the beginning of time. God has a master plan and there is no stopping the divine will of God! We are in the army of God, and there is a war raging.

> *Yea, and all that will live godly in Christ Jesus shall suffer persecution* (II Timothy 3:12).

This is a definite statement from the Lord. Those who try to say we will get out of here before any trouble comes are missing something. We *will* have to fight the enemy and become overcomers in Him, or we will not be a part of that glorious Church.

I gave you the message to the Church with the instructions for setting a watch, now I want to give you the steps to enable you to carry out those instructions:

1. Arise out of slumber

> *Therefore let us not sleep as do others; but let us watch and be sober* (I Thessalonians 5:6).

The Church has been nothing more than a sleeping giant in the world for generations. The Lord is saying to us now, **wake up**! Arise out of slumber and pay attention to what is happening around you. The word, *sober,* in this text means "discreet," which means "be careful about what you say and do." Does that give new insight into the instruction of watching and being sober?

2. Be Constantly On Guard

Not every one that saith unto Me, Lord, Lord, shall enter into the kingdom of heaven; but he that doeth the will of My Father which is in heaven (Matthew 7:21).

We know that the devil is a deceiver and has been from the beginning. His job is to kill, steal and destroy the lives of the children of God. We must learn to discern the spirits and see if they are of God. *Try the spirits.* There is a spirit of *naiveté* that is running rampant in the Church today. If someone declares to be of the Lord, then, *who are we to pass judgment on that*? The Word tells us to *try the spirits.* The Word also tells us we will know them by their fruit. Is the fruit good? *Is it fruit that remains?* If not, then be on guard and hear the Spirit of the Lord speaking to your spirit.

3. We must be "doers" of the Word

But be ye doers of the Word, and not hearers only, deceiving your own selves (James 1:22).

If we hear the Word and go out into our every day life and don't apply what we have heard, *we will fail*! We will not be victorious in the battles of life. We need to realize that life is what happens to us on our way to where we are going. Jesus wants us to realize that the Gospel is applicable to our now. He is a *now* God!

4. We must clothe ourselves with righteousness

And to her was granted that she should be arrayed in fine linen, clean and white; for the fine linen is the righteousness of the saints (Revelation 19:8).

How do we get this righteousness? It's the righteousness of Christ. We are told to put on our breastplate of righteousness which is a part of His armor (Ephesians 6:14). He supplies it, but *we must put it on*!

5. Be careful not to be encumbered with the cares of this life.

And take heed to yourselves, lest at any time your hearts be overcharged with surfeiting, and drunkenness, and cares of this life, and so that day come upon you unawares. For as a snare shall it come on all them that dwell on the face of the whole earth. Watch ye therefore, and pray always, that ye may be accounted worthy to escape all these things that shall come to pass, and to stand before the Son of Man (Luke 21:34-36).

This is the only place in the Bible the word *surfeiting* is used. It means "debauch or glut," which means "to morally lead astray or extreme indulgence in appetite."

Is this an important instruction or what? Be careful not to be overcome with the cares of this life. *Get yourself unencumbered!* Why are these instructions so important in this Last Day preparation? So we won't be unprepared. So we won't become entangled. So we won't be deceived! So we'll escape the judgment and be able to stand before the *Son of Man*. Watching and praying is not a matter of choice—it is a matter of survival!

Therefore let us not sleep, as do others; but let us watch and be sober (I Thessalonians 5:6).

The Lord is so faithful to give us all that we need to be overcomers in Him, to be victorious children of the King. We are in the army now, and *we are career soldiers*. We must realize that we didn't come in for just a stint in the army; it is our life!

The Lord gave me a prophetic word some time ago pertaining to this last day. I have called it:

The Eye of the Storm

At this time in church history, there is a storm brewing; a wind of such high velocity, that only those who are spiritually prepared will survive. There will be chaos, havoc and destruction; but there will also be a place of peace and protection. There will be a holy hush and a calm of such magnitude that the very breath of God will be heard by those who have entered the eye of the storm. I believe it is then that we will hear the Bride say, "Come."

Chapter 19

That's the Bride Wearing Combat Boots

And His wife hath made herself ready (Revelation 19:7).

As I look at the Body of Christ in the various places I travel, and in the everyday circumstances of life, I see such an array of parts; some will become part of the Bride, and some will not. I see those who are soldiers who are MIA's. They are *missing in action*. They have been given something to work with—a gifting or calling—and have not used it. The Lord tells us that if we do not use what He entrusts us with, He will give it to someone who will. (See the parable of the talents in Luke 19.)

Then there are those who are AWOL. They just can't seem to take orders. They have no respect for authority and choose to do their own thing. They think they can get back into the swing of things whenever they choose; but, sadly, they find a sentence of prison waiting for them if they do not get back in time.

135

But, I think the saddest of all are the POW's. These are the ones who have been on the battlefield. Many of them have been on the front lines in the realm of the Spirit and have taken more than one enemy bullet. Then the enemy comes into their camp with *pride, sin, temptation, lust, power, wealth* and whatever he can get to work against them, and they fall for the lie. They become a prisoner of war and the devil gets them to believe they can never be restored to their rightful place in the army of God. They are beaten up and left to die many times by their own people. It has been said that the army of God is the only army in the world who kills its wounded. How many MIA's, AWOL's or POW's in the army of God are out there? It's time for the Bride to put her combat boots on and go to war!

The Lord gave me a description of the Bride wearing combat boots. He said she is: *pure,* but *powerful; strong,* but *sensitive; beautiful* but *bold; and meek* but *mighty.*

I looked up the meanings of these words in the dictionary and received great insight as to what the Lord was really saying to me about His Bride.

1. Pure

Means "free from anything that taints, impairs, infects or adulterates (meaning to make impure); free from guilt or sin; virgin or chaste" (*Webster's New World Dictionary of the American Language,* 123).

Powerful

Means "having much power. Strong, mighty, influential or effective."

2. Strong

Means "not easily defeated, morally powerful, having strength of character or will, able to resist and endure attack."

Sensitive

Means "tender, emotions easily moved by actions of others, responding or feeling readily or acutely, affected by light."

3. Beautiful

Means "that which has beauty; beautiful is applied to that which gives the highest degree of pleasure to the senses or to the mind and suggests that the object of delight approximates one's conception of an ideal." (It just doesn't get any better than this!)

Bold

Means "showing a readiness to face danger or take risks, fearless."

4. Meek

Means "gentle, pliant, patient and mild, not easily inclined to anger or resentment."

Mighty

Means "having might, remarkably large, extensive, great, very extremely."

What a description of the Bride of Christ! As I looked at the attributes the Lord spoke to me, I had to start inspecting myself to see which ones were missing, or what I have in my life that will please my soon-to-come Bridegroom. Our heart must be to please Him.

The Lord then gave me a poem to describe the Bride wearing combat boots:

The Bride Wearing Combat Boots

Yes, she's pure but powerful, and beautiful but bold,
  The Bride wearing combat boots, that's a sight to behold.
She follows Her orders, to reach out in love,
  To a world of lost victims that don't know His Love.
Though strong but sensitive, she's mighty but meek,
  She marches to battle for lost souls to seek.
Her gown's without blemish, pure, holy and white,
  Her eyes are on Jesus, for He is her Light.
Marching through battles and ne'er losing sight,
  Of the victories waiting, when wrong yields to right.
The Bride will wear her combat boots, take on all trials and tests,
  Fight through the darkest jungle to bring in wedding guests.
She knows it will be worth it, for that day is coming soon,
  All the fighting will be over, and she will see her Groom.

Prepared for the wedding, prepared for the war. That's **the bride wearing combat boots**!

Chapter 20

The Vision of the Vials

I will pour out My Spirit upon all flesh (Joel 2:28).

As I close this writing, I want to share with you one of the most frightening and exciting visions I have ever been given. I trust you will enter into this vision with me, so you can be prepared to take your rightful place in His Body as part of His Bride.

The Vision

I was sitting in my living room with my Bible on my lap. I had been asking the Lord to give me some insight into various things I was reading in His Word. I read where there would be a mighty outpouring of His Spirit in the last day like had never been know to man, with the former and latter day rains combined. I also read that there would be a great falling away from the Body of Christ before His return. In my finite mind, I couldn't comprehend how this could happen all at the same time. I

139

know the Word tells us if we lack wisdom to ask of God and He will give us what we need, so I asked!

The next thing I knew, I was standing in the middle of a room. The walls were lined with shelves, and the floor, the walls, the ceiling—everything in the room was made from the most beautiful wood I have ever seen.

On the shelves and sitting all over the floor were all kinds of jars and vases and various containers, all with lids of some kind on them. Some of the lids seemed to be like cork stoppers, while others seemed to be screw-on lids that matched the containers. The colors of these containers were beautiful beyond description. The blues and greens and reds were unlike anything I had ever seen before.

I could see three walls from where I was standing. All at once, I felt a presence behind me. I turned around and found myself facing the largest angel I could ever imagine. He was standing in the middle of the doorway, and his presence filled the entire space in the door. He had on what I describe as a Roman soldier uniform that seemed to be pure gold. Even his countenance seemed to be golden.

At his side was a sword in a sheath. The sword appeared to be a flame of fire. As I looked at this, my natural mind wondered if that fire was burning his leg. I thought I must be dreaming or something, but this sure did seem to be real. As I was pondering exactly what was happening, I heard what sounded to me like thunder. . . Again, I heard the thunder. . . Then, the third time, the angel pulled the flaming sword from his side and began to swing it around the room. The sound of WHOOOOOSH. . . as it seemed to fly over my head brought fear to my heart. I thought, "My God, I'm going to die." As I raised my hands to protect myself from this flame, I heard the sound of "POP, POP, POP" all around me.

I didn't know what was going on, but as I looked up, I saw the lids and stoppers flying off the jars and vials and vases all around me. Out of the various sized containers came vapors of the most breathtaking fragrance I had ever encountered. I thought, "My God, what is this? What is happening?"

Instantly, the scene changed, and I found myself standing on what I knew to be a street corner in downtown Columbus, Ohio. Now, I don't go to downtown Columbus very often—mostly because I'm not sure I'd find my way back home (you know how I am with directions).

Standing on this corner, I am wondering what is going to happen next. I feel in my spirit that I'm to take in the scenes around me and pay attention to what is happening.

At the curb, there's a long, black car. Leaning in the passenger's window is a woman dressed in the most peculiar way. Her back is to me, but I can see the lace leotards on her legs, the black leather mini skirt and the bra-like top under a long black-laced jacket. She has long black hair and she is laughing at something the man in the car has said to her. She then turns around, and I can see through all the heavy makeup that she is only about 16 years of age. I thought to myself, "What in the world is a young girl like this doing out on the street this time of night?"

I thought she must be cold in that outfit she had on, but she didn't seem to notice the weather. She walked over to a man standing at the corner waiting to cross the street. She put her arm through his and began to laugh and talk to him in a seductive manner. It was then that I realized she was a prostitute, and the man was her client for the night.

As I looked on this scene, my heart was overwhelmed with the pain I felt for this young girl. All at once, a vapor (like the ones that came out of the vials) came down around her. It began at her head and completely encircled her down to her feet. Her head fell into her hands and she became overwrought with emotion. She began to weep uncontrollable, sobbing and shaking all over. The man looked at her, and it was like I could see his thoughts: he had gotten a real wacko this time. She raised up her head, and her makeup was running all down her face. She looked at her outfit as though it were the first time in her life she had ever seen it and said, "My God, what have I done? Look at me! *What have I done?*"

She then turned and began to run down the street. It was as though I was right with her. She ran up the steps of a huge stone church standing on the corner. There were people going in the church as though there was a wedding or a program of some kind going on that night. At the door stood what I took to be the minister of this church. He had on a very expensive looking suit and such shiny shoes: they just seemed to stand out! He reached in front of the young girl to stop her from entering the church and said, "Where do you think you're going?" She said, "I've got to find God! *Look at me!* I've got to find God!"

"Not in my church!" he said, and pointed to the street for her to leave. She ran down the steps weeping, saying to herself, "Where can I go? What can I do?" She then said, "I know! I'll go to that little old lady's house who tried to get me to come in to visit her for so long. The one who always tells me Jesus loves me when I pass by."

Though she had thought for so long that this little grandma was kinda crazy, she now knew the old woman would have the answer she was looking for. She ran down the street and through the gate to a little house which seemed so insignificant to its surroundings. A little white-haired lady opened the door and said, "Come on in honey, I've been waiting for you."

Immediately, I was back in my living room, *wondering what in the world had just happened.* I knew I had not been sleeping. I also knew the Lord was giving me a revelation that I wasn't sure I could comprehend.

As I sat there almost in a daze, the Holy Spirit began to speak to me. He said I had been shown the vials of the prayers of the saints which are yet to be answered. He told me that just as there had been a time set from the foundation of the world for Jesus to be born; just as there was a time set for Him to die and raise from the grave; just as surely, there is a set time for Him to come again. He let me know there are prayers which, from the foundation of the world, were meant to be *last-day answers.* He let me know the young girl represents all those who are in sin, who have a mother or grandmother or father or brother praying for them to come into the saving grace of Jesus Christ before it is too late.

The vapors are the prayers of the saints who are waiting for the voice of the Father (the thunderings) to speak to the keeper of the vials, to let them go.

The minister at the church door represents the *last-day dead religion* which will refuse to allow in the Spirit of God. And the little grandmother represents the ministering body of Christ Jesus whom He is getting ready to go into all the world and preach the Gospel before His return. It will be a *great outpouring of His Spirit*; but at the same time a *great falling away*.

The Lord then said that the last-day revival will bring in the pimps, the pushers, the prostitutes, the drug addicts and all the downtrodden of the earth. Why? Because the *vials of the prayers of the saints are about to be opened.*

And when he had taken the book, the four beasts and the four and twenty elders fell down before the Lamb, having every one of them harps and golden vials full of odors, which are the prayers of the saints (Revelation 5:8).

Who are going to be able to minister to all these new saints of God? It will be the one who is prepared for the wedding, prepared for the war. That's the bride wearing combat boots!

Epilogue

I don't know what the Lord has in store for us tomorrow. The Soul Seekers Evangelistic Association has received so many prophetic words, so many promises; some from the Lord, some from the flesh. But, I do know this: I don't want to seek after the promises, the gifts or the manifestations of His Spirit, I want to seek after Him!

Lord, let my prayer always be, "That I may know Him and the power of His resurrection and the fellowship of His sufferings, being made conformable even unto His death."

Pastor Kelly Varner, in his book *Whose Right It Is* wrote something that really spoke to my heart. He said, "All spiritual warfare must be waged from the posture of Jesus' finished work. Our Lord rests within the rent veil, the enthroned ruler over all enemies. Unless we stand and fight from the perspective of solid resurrection ground, we will continue to do no more than cover ourselves with sweat and beat the air."

Lord, let me be an effective witness for Your kingdom and for Your glory. Amen!

May the Lord use the truths of this book to encourage, enlighten and enhance the Bride of Christ as she goes forth.

Prepared for the wedding,
prepared for the war.
Yes, that's the bride
wearing combat boots!

Afterword

I have learned so much from the writings, ministries, and lives of so many people throughout the years. Kathryn Kuhlman's life was such an inspiration to me along with Oswald Chambers, Alfred Goodrich Garr, and Aimee Simple McPhearson—just to name a few that have gone on to be with the Lord. Of those that are ministering today, the writings and teachings of people like Margaret Jensen, Don Nori, Roy Ralph, and the entire team from Morning Star Ministries, especially Rick Joyner and Steve Thompson, have truly been a source of inspiration throughout the years. I would be amiss if I failed to also mention Brother Wade Taylor from Pinecrest Bible Institute, who has truly been an instrument in the hands of the Lord to inspire and encourage me to become all the Lord created me to be. My prayer is that I will be able to convey the things I have learned from others without crossing over that dreaded fine line of plagiarism.

May those who read this book take the truths that I have written and, in turn, minister them to others.

To God be the glory. . . .

For more information on music or teaching tapes
or to schedule the
Soul Seekers Evangelistic Association
for a concert or revival call:
740-246-5212
or write:
S.S.E.A.
c/o Evangelist Lois A. Hoshor
P.O. Box 547
Thornville, OH 43076-0547